Blackwell's Practical Guides for Teachers

Education and Philosophy

Blackwell's Practical Guides for Teachers

Education and Philosophy
A Practical Approach

KEITH THOMPSON

OXFORD · BASIL BLACKWELL

Printed in Great Britain by
Western Printing Services Ltd, Bristol
and bound by The Kemp Hall Bindery, Oxford

To be a philosopher is to philosophize and the function of a philosophical book is to help people to philosophize for themselves.

(David Pears on Wittgenstein's view)

The most important thing about a philosopher's arguments is that it should be as easy as possible . . . to catch him out if he can be caught out.

(Gilbert Ryle)

I wish to thank those who have read the book in draft and have caught me out, but extend to them the courtesy of anonymity lest they be found guilty by association with remaining weaknesses. This is particularly necessary because of the degree to which I have resisted some of their criticisms.

CONTENTS

Preface   ix

1. Philosophies and Philosophy: the nature of educational problems   1

2. Evidence and Criteria   9

3. Further consideration of the nature of Philosophy   16

4. Meaning and Language   22

5. Play and natural development   28

6. Teaching and the Teacher   39

7. The Curriculum   50

8. Subject-centred and child-centred theories   60

9. The 'Aims' of Education   78

10. The Disciplines of Education   89

11. Educational Institutions: Discipline, Freedom, Authority and Responsibility   105

12. Education and Society: Freedom, Authority and Responsibility   126

13. Education and Society: Equality and Democracy 133

14. Further Issues
    (1) The nature of intelligence 147
    (2) How far can streaming be justified? 153
    (3) How should secondary education be organized? 157
    (4) What is indoctrination? 161

15. Conclusion 166

    Bibliography 168

PREFACE

'Education' is now generally considered to be important and educational developments, changes and controversies are newsworthy. It has not always been so. When education was the preserve of the few it was not the concern of the many. And even since the gradual development of popular education (in England State-initiative, as opposed to State-aid, dates only from 1870) it has been generally true that much educational development has taken place within the bounds of professional concern and not in the spotlight of public discussion. The 'lower orders' would not have thought themselves fitted to comment on method or content.

But it is in the nature of the educational process that it will create its own momentum. As gradually people are taught to be critical, they will turn their criticism to education itself. And in a society in which educational provision is universal its importance will come to be perceived, however hazily, and the changes which take place within it will cease to be the preserve of the few.

This book is designed primarily for all those who, believing education to be important, wish not only to find out more about it but to be able to think clearly about that which they find out. In one sense there is little problem about the 'finding out' itself. The press, radio, television—all mass media are much occupied with giving information and advice to parents and teachers, and the bookshops and bookstalls have many publications designed to guide and inform. In some cases it may be clear that expert knowledge is needed to interpret the information, for example knowledge of the correct interpretation of statistics. But frequently what may be felt to be lacking is any general procedure for distinguishing the valid from the invalid, for assessing the force or relevance of a case. One authoritative pronouncement is countered by another, apparently equally authoritative, claiming precisely the opposite.

There is, of course, no single formula which can help to, let alone be guaranteed to answer all educational problems. But a great deal can be achieved by considering what kinds of problems these are. And in setting about this task there are a number of techniques, derived from philosophy, which are coming to be applied more and more widely. It is my firm belief that these can be used by anyone seriously concerned to think purposefully and rationally about educational issues. Because they are philosophical techniques, it does not follow that they are abstruse or that they are confined to a few experts, who combine the image of the sage with that of total impracticability. They can be used by parents, teachers and students and they can be used to help deal with practical problems. It is with the use of such techniques that this book is concerned.

Keith Thompson has been Head of the Education Department at Philippa Fawcett College of Education, London, since 1967. Since 1968 he has also been Editor of 'Education for Teaching'.

1. PHILOSOPHIES AND PHILOSOPHY

The nature of educational problems

My aim in this book is not to give the reader a set of guiding values against which to judge educational provision and educational claims. I am concerned with the ways in which one thinks about educational issues, not, in the popular sense, with 'what I think about them'. Indeed, part of my concern is with consideration of which elements in discussions about education are ones which can be shown to be true or untrue and which remain open to personal opinion or judgment. To put this another way, I am concerned with helping others to build their own philosophy of education by investigating the nature of the parts of the educational process and their relationship to one another. This book is a set of guidelines for the reader to build his thinking about education; it is neither an existing model nor a kit with all the parts, requiring only that they should be assembled.

In ordinary usage the word 'philosophy' suggests a system of values or an outlook on life. This is a perfectly acceptable use of the term. And it is used in this sense within educational discussion. Thus we might say of someone that he had a traditional philosophy of education, or a Christian philosophy of education or a child-centred philosophy of education. To say this kind of thing is to make a form of shorthand summary of his basic attitudes towards education. From such a statement one might be prepared to infer an elaborated set of statements concerning various values which he would support, procedures he would be likely to adopt, ends he would regard as important and moves he would oppose.

Anyone whose advocacy is wide-ranging and consistent has a philosophy in this sense. And it is a very important sense. Certainly I have a philosophy of education of this kind. For example, I believe in the importance of rationality, I believe in maintaining a broad curriculum for a long period in the secondary school, I believe in treating questions of value as open to discussion, I believe that too little attention is paid to political education in schools, I believe that more time should be spent on teaching children how to think in various areas and less emphasis placed on particular content. These are some examples. But the fact that I happen to believe in these things is in itself of little significance. What is of importance is the question of the grounds upon which I would defend my belief in them.

It might here be pointed out that one of the elements I quoted as among my beliefs was the importance of rationality, and that I am presuming this when I say that the grounds of my belief, the reasons which I would give to support it, are more important than the belief itself. This is true. But it is unavoidable. For even to ask me why I believe this, is to ask for reasons and thus to presuppose my readiness to give them. Anyone who seriously asks why I believe a certain thing is likewise assuming the importance of being able to give reasons. Of course one might reply 'I just believe it, that's all' or 'I feel it in my bones; I can't say why' or 'anyone who doesn't believe that is a fool'. But a direct confrontation of beliefs of this kind, by definition, allows no means of assessment of them.

So it *is* my presumption that beliefs and value positions should be reasoned about. And it is this element in my own personal philosophy of education which enables me to help to

2

construct a framework within which further philosophizing can take place. But it is the latter which is crucial. I wish to help to produce more practitioners not to hand over pre-packed thoughts. I wish to help people to solve educational problems and to do this I shall have to stress the importance of examining closely the status of claims made within educational discourse so as to discover what is required to substantiate them. This, in turn, will lead to consideration of some of the presuppositions which frequently lie hidden and to a close examination of the language within which the claims are made.

If we are to solve educational problems we must understand what *kind* of problem we are trying to solve. So let us begin there. One answer might seem to be that there is scarcely a question; one has said what kind of problem when one has said 'educational'. But this needs looking at more closely. Suppose, by contrast, that I were to say that I was trying to solve a mathematical problem. To say this is to give some fairly clear indication of the type of problem. One could still ask 'what kind of mathematical problem?' but the answer to this would be a sub-division of mathematics, for example 'an algebraic problem'.

Now if I were to ask 'what kind of educational problem?' it is not at all clear what answer would be likely to be given. It would seem that the most likely form would be a reference to the actual problem; for example, 'one concerning the organization of secondary schooling'. Put another way, my point is that to call a problem 'educational' seems to be to refer to the *context* within which it arises rather than to the *type* of problem that it is. Educational problems have to do with teaching and learning, with teachers and children, with schools and pupils. To say this, however, says nothing about the way in which they are to be solved. Mathematical problems are solved by mathematical methods; if they are algebraic

3

problems they are solved by algebraic methods. But what could be an educational method of solving an educational problem? Or a secondary school method of solving a problem about secondary schools?

It can now be seen fairly clearly that the methods by which educational problems are solved involve seeing what types of problem are posed within them. Rather than trying to list or categorize these in general at this stage, let me take as an example an actual question likely to be asked within education by parents and teachers, indeed by anyone generally interested: 'What is the best method for teaching a child to read?' I take this, I repeat, only as an example. But it is a question which is likely to be asked and, on the surface at any rate, it looks comparatively simple *as a question*; that is it seems quite clear what is being asked, however much doubt there may be about the answer.

But is the question so clear? First, it is worth asking what, if anything, is presumed by a questioner before the question is asked. In this case there would seem to be a presumption that a child should learn to read. In our world this may seem unexceptionable, but let us at least note that the presumption is there. There may be other questions, similar in form, where the presumption of the worthwhile nature of the end would by no means always command assent. Having granted this, it might look like a simple means-to-end argument. 'Reading' is the end. The method which 'best' achieves it is the best method. And the problem becomes one for practical experiment. But it is far from being so simple.

One could well enquire what it is for a child to be able to read. It is clearly not a single point of achievement. Certainly children move from a stage at which they cannot read at all to one at which they can read difficult material with fluency, expression and, within their vocabulary, understanding—or

4

some of them do. But there is nowhere along the line where one can with confidence make a cut-off mark and say 'at this point "reading" is achieved'. Realizing this, it can be seen that there may well be methods of teaching reading which, for example, get certain quick results but entail long-run difficulties, while others produce greater difficulties at first but establish a firm base for later progress. Which then are the 'best'? Or suppose that Method A seems to score in effectiveness over Method B by almost every measure which is used, except that a large number of children dislike Method A and few dislike Method B. Which then is the better? Or suppose that one method produces great speed and fluency but low comprehension of the material. Is this method adequate? Does a child have to understand what he is reading for us to say that he is reading? Or suppose that one method is more helpful to the child's learning of spelling and thus to his accuracy of writing. Is this to be counted in its favour even as a method of learning *reading*?

It is vital to be quite clear at this stage what I am pointing out. I repeat—this is an *example*. I am not saying that any of my suggestions are in fact true of methods of reading. What I am pointing out is that the issues may arise and yet, at first sight, it looked as though the question being asked—'What is the best method for teaching a child to read?'—was a simple question.

The possible complexities have been far from exhausted however. The queries I have raised have been general ones about the meaning which might be given to 'best' and the ambiguity which lurks in 'reading'. But there are also particular questions. Which child? At what age? In the hands of which teacher? Some children may respond better to one method than another. Some may respond better to one at one age and to another later on. And one method may suit the general approach of a particular teacher better than another (there are writers on education who speak as though individual differences between children are a wonderful opportunity but between teachers are a wretched nuisance!).

If one combines these variable elements it is clear that the 'straightforward' question looks complicated indeed, even before questions are asked about what evidence is available in helping us to come to conclusions. Yet even at this stage we have over-simplified by supposing that there is a clear range of distinct methods, whereas in fact there may be any number of overlapping ones with varying emphases.

This initial example establishes certain points before the argument proceeds any further. First, educational questions may well break down into a number of sub-questions of very different kinds. Second, these sub-questions demand different approaches before they can be answered. Third, these approaches seem to involve questions of fact—of what actually happens in certain circumstances, questions of meaning—of what we are taking particular terms to refer to, and questions of value—of what we regard as good or important.

Given that education is regarded as important, a great deal of advocacy is bound to be indulged in within it. What is often confusing, when one seeks to find out about an educational issue, is that the information in the area concerned is so often purveyed by someone who is also concerned with advocating a particular viewpoint. The reader, or listener, is thus frequently unsure whether he can rely on the information which he is given and the analysis which is made of the issues under discussion. Has the advocacy arisen from the facts and the analysis or have these been educed in order to support a position which had already been adopted? Indeed, how far is it possible to separate the elements in this way?

From even this glimpse of the general situation, it may be

seen why it is so vitally important that *all* parents, teachers and indeed citizens within a democratic society should have considerable insight into educational issues. Parents have to take complex and far-reaching decisions regarding the education of their children; teachers are involved in decisions about both means and ends constantly; the electorate as a whole has to pronounce upon educational questions at the polls, and, in a healthy democracy, many will do so through associations and groups of various kinds. 'Education is too important to leave to the experts' might be one way of putting the point, but it is an inadequate one, for it does nothing to illuminate the nature of the importance. Many important matters are left to the experts. But, as I have begun to show, educational questions are a complex amalgam of varying expertise with judgments of 'what matters'. And in this, as a whole, each must become his own judge. To show fully why I believe this, this introductory sketch does not suffice. The rest of the book both presupposes it and, in many ways, continues to argue it.

Before continuing the case, however, a word of warning. I have stated that I believe that there are techniques which can help anyone seriously interested and concerned to think more cogently about educational issues. This must not be taken as equivalent to saying that there is an easy way *through*. There is an effective and not, I think, too difficult way *in*. But the results of using it are to show that the issues with which we are faced are complex in the extreme and that really mastering them involves great persistence.

I aim to give some understanding of certain broad approaches. A little learning is a dangerous thing only when it is mistaken for much learning. There will be only slight danger of this happening in this area. But the basic understanding will give some protection against the slick operators who place

7

on the market educational panaceas for all social ills. There are no such panaceas. This book is written for those who wish to face perplexities but also to have to have some idea of how to unravel them. It is not for those who wish to side-step them.

2. EVIDENCE AND CRITERIA

'What I should really like to know are the facts'. Frequently one hears some comment of this kind in a discussion about education. It sounds appealing. There is a suggestion that the mists of prejudice and the storm clouds of controversy might be swept away if only the facts were known. How much more reliable than mere opinion. We all know what we think, or perhaps what we feel, but what can we know? Facts; hard gritty facts; unarguable, undisputable, carefully verified facts —throw these into the arena and all will be well. The media frequently play on this desire: 'You are confused by the conflicting opinions which surround the question of comprehensive schools? The Daily * has been investigating the question and begins its report on the facts on Monday'. Hopes are raised. But often disappointment follows. One seems no clearer with 'the facts' than one was without them. From them no policy seems necessarily to follow. And, in any case, the Daily *'s correspondence column is quickly taken up with letters which deny that the alleged facts are facts at all.

Even apparently simple and straightforward statements of fact may conceal unsuspected problems. Take, for example, the statement that there are three primary schools in Bridgebury. This is true if there are three primary schools in Bridgebury and false if there are not. This would seem to be a very simple statement of fact. How does one verify that it is true? The obvious response, I suppose, is to say that one goes to Bridgebury and looks. Or one might rest content with looking it up in a reference list or with phoning the local library and enquiring or with contacting the Education Officer for the area in which Bridgebury was situated.

Even so simple a fact as this however might involve certain complications. One needs a clear definition of a 'primary school'. Suppose that this is taken to be a school catering for children up to the age of eleven. And suppose that in Bridgebury there are two schools combining infants (5–7) and juniors (8–11), one infant school and one junior school. Thus there are four primary schools in Bridgebury. Though true, this may be misleading. The infant school which is separate, sends all its children, normally, to the junior school which draws only from there. For some purposes it might be more helpful to refer to three primary schools in Bridgebury. And suppose that there is also a small private, fee-paying, school for pupils up to the age of eleven. Do we include this or not? The answer is that it depends on our purpose. When the Director of Education makes a return he does not count it in. But if a well-to-do family move into the area they may regard it as relevant, or, indeed, as the vital factor.

Thus it can be seen that even a fact so disarmingly simple is context-dependent and definition-dependent. What counts as a primary school depends upon one's purposes. It may well seem that little confusion is likely to arise over this, and that, if there is some confusion in a particular situation, it will soon be sorted out. But this is to misunderstand the point, which is that if there can be confusion over something so concrete and particular and if definition in this area is dependent upon context and purpose, how much more likely it is that similar difficulties will arise in more complex and abstract areas and how much less likely that they will be easily resolved.

Take another example; it is a fact that John Jones came top of his class last term. This may be a clear statement of fact. John Jones' class teacher produced a list which showed the class in order and John's name was at the head of the list; his school report said that he was first in his class. In this case the problem is not with the fact itself but with its interpretation. In isolation it may be a true statement that John Jones was the top of his class. But when we want to know what is in fact the case, we also want to know the significance of the fact. And this is much harder to judge. Here are some questions almost at random. What is the general standard of work like in John's school? Which class is John in? Is the school 'streamed' (i.e. are the classes separated by some measure of ability)? Which areas of work were covered by the marks in question? How were the marks arrived at? Do any of them involve the teacher's estimate? How does John's age compare with that of his classmates? Was there a different weighting of different areas of work? Were marks given for effort? Were marks given for tidiness? And so on . . . . the reader may like to add to the list. The *fact* is simple. It is concerned with one child on one occasion. But to gain any educational significance from the fact (and what help is it to us otherwise?) a string of further questions has to be asked.

A further example: x% of candidates in subject Y passed at O level. A fact. But its significance? How many passed with other examining boards? How many passed in other subjects? And for 'how many' should I have substituted 'what percentage'? What percentage passed the previous year? Has there been a rise in the entry? Is there any policy on what percentage should pass? Again one could continue the questions; from the fact alone nothing follows.

If isolated facts are so unhelpful, one may wonder what might follow from a body of facts, from what one may call 'the evidence' in a particular area. Two initial suppositions might be made, apparently contrary ones. One would be that if such difficulties arise with particular statements of fact they are likely to arise far more acutely with a body of evidence, for the problems will be repeated again and again. On the other hand it might be argued that the body of evidence can take into account the mass of questions stimulated by any particular statement of fact and thus give us the whole picture, free from confusion, doubt and ambiguity.

To consider the matter let us work through an example again. Suppose that we want to know the facts concerning the relative forms of secondary school organization. We know that there is a mass of controversy, of advocacy and counteradvocacy, of radical urgings and passionate defence of the status quo. It seems reasonable to ask for the facts. But for what facts is one asking? What facts are relevant to the issue in question?

One might wish perhaps to make comparisons between comprehensive schools and grammar schools. The facts could be concerned with numbers of pupils, staffing ratios, values held to be important within the schools, average I.Q.s, range of subjects taught, teaching methods employed, academic results in terms of O levels, A levels, University entrance, and so on. But the essential point about the facts in any context of educational discussion is that use is made of them. The facts are wanted in order to know what is the case and, in turn, to make decisions about what should or should not be done in some respect. In other words, though the facts themselves are inert, the selection and organization of the facts which matter, those which are relevant, presuppose a view of the situation.

In any large scale issue one cannot begin to select the facts without some grounds of selection. And seeking for these is likely immediately to open up difficulties and controversy.

Nevertheless, it remains true that the evidence may have some of the virtues of objectivity. Statements of fact can be checked against the facts themselves. And if anyone feels that the selection with which they are faced is biased and partial, or that false interpretations are being placed upon the facts, then it is open for them to seek for further evidence and to argue for its relevance.

It is crucial however to note that any request for evidence presupposes some agreement on criteria; it is the failure to realize this that renders the demand for the facts naïve from the very outset, if it is thought that these are self-selecting and guaranteed against misunderstanding.

In the particular examples cited we saw that we needed to know a definition of 'primary school', the measure by which John Jones was top of the class, what constituted a pass at O level. And to compare comprehensive schools with grammar schools we need definitions of both which are agreed. A more technical way of making the point is that we need agreement on the criteria in accordance with which a particular category of objects or events is being picked out, or a particular object or event identified.

A further example: suppose that we are interested in the connection between broken homes and juvenile delinquency. It might seem that there is a fairly simple factual question which could be asked: 'what percentage of juvenile delinquents come from broken homes?' But no *meaningful* answer could be given to it at all unless there were agreement on the criteria in accordance with which a home was deemed to be 'broken' and a juvenile to be 'delinquent'—and we need to know the criteria for 'juvenile' too (and for 'home'?). This point is basic and exceedingly important; it is not just that it helps to clarify these points, it is that without clarifying them there is no way of producing any facts—any evidence—at all.

Every request for the facts presupposes criteria. How clever is Mary?—what are the criteria in accordance with which cleverness is being assessed? Can Robert read?—what constitutes 'reading'? Does Jane know her five times table?—what do you mean by know? Is reciting it enough? How much hesitation is allowed before an answer? Does one 'dodge about' with the questions? Does she have to *understand* what multiplication is?)

There may be problems of criteria even in a question which at first sight appears wholly free of them. How many children are in Mr. Brown's class? Does this mean are officially 'on the register'? Probably it does, but for some purposes this might be very misleading; the questioner might really want to know how many children Mr. Brown normally has to deal with, but Mr. Brown might have added several new names to the register in the previous few days knowing that several other children were about to leave.

Some of my examples may appear strained. But the point of them is to emphasize that if hidden traps are present in the most innocuous of 'factual statements', there are likely to be crucial and subtle traps of the same sort in the more complex and abstract phrases of educational controversy. 'How much freedom should children be allowed?' 'Education should aim at social equality'. 'Children should be grouped in accordance with their intelligence'. 'Academic excellence must be preserved at all costs'. How can any judgment of any worth be made about this type of question or claim until the criteria for the application of the key terms are agreed? What is meant by freedom, social equality, intelligence, academic excellence?

All questions regarding facts, therefore, presuppose grounds for selecting these facts as being relevant to the question in hand and presuppose also criteria in accordance with which the key terms are to be applied. Not only do they presuppose these elements but they also generate many questions of interpretation. A call for 'the facts' is naïve if it is taken to imply that when the facts are forthcoming we shall know what we ought to do. For, beyond the facts, the criteria, the interpretations, lie the evaluations—the judgments of what each of us regards as important. And these cannot be deduced from the facts. The facts of a situation always leave open various possibilities for action. They may rule out certain policies, show that they could not be carried through successfully, but they do not make any policies inevitable. Whatever is the case, many different things may be done about it. So, in judging educational questions, there are certain kinds of phrases which should always set a red warning light flashing in our minds; phrases such as 'the evidence makes it clear that we ought . . .', 'in the light of the facts it is quite clear that we must . . .', 'given the reality of the situation there is no alternative but to . . .'. To questions of value I shall return in more detail later. I have said sufficient to indicate that educational discussion normally involves some statement of the facts and some evaluation and recommendation.

With the facts as such this book is not concerned. It is time to consider more explicitly the nature of philosophy and the particular contributions which it can make. In my analysis so far some of the points have been philosophical in nature. I shall now discuss further the nature of philosophical argument and begin to illustrate how it can help towards the resolution of educational problems. I must repeat, however, that this book is not itself concerned with the solution of problems directly. The examples I use are to be taken *as examples*. The aim of the book is to give an understanding of the issues involved. Even here it cannot give all the approaches necessary. But I believe that the philosophical approach is crucial and it is my intention to show why I believe this and to help others to make use of it.

3. FURTHER CONSIDERATION OF THE NATURE OF PHILOSOPHY

Philosophy of education is concerned, as I stated earlier, with an examination of the nature and structure of educational arguments. It is uniquely concerned with those questions in education where we are unclear as to what constitutes an answer. It must be noted immediately that I have not said 'where we do not know the answer'. This distinction needs explanation.

If I am asked how many eleven-year-old children in Middlesbrough are being taught by teachers who are in their probationary year, I do not know the answer. But I know how to find out and how to verify the truth of the answer (subject to agreed criteria). But if I am asked whether immigrant children should be taught English in smaller classes than normal, there is a lack of clarity about what constitutes an answer. Of course I could say 'no, they shouldn't' or 'yes, they should', but the question suggests that an answer is required which gives grounds to justify it. And one may be unsure what constitutes justification here. Or suppose that one is asked what indoctrination is. I might give a dictionary definition but be told—'oh, yes, I know that this is roughly what it means but I want to know what it *really* is.' What constitutes an adequate answer to this? Or I might be asked what the real purposes of education are, or whether music can be justified as a subject in the curriculum, or what every human being should understand. Many people would be prepared to offer answers to this kind of question but there are doubts about what is wanted as a reply. This is not just to say 'about what reply is wanted' but rather 'about what *kind* of reply is wanted'.

It may be that some of the questions have no answers. Are there grounds for teaching immigrants English in smaller classes which are more than just opinion?—or for not doing so? Has indoctrination a *real* meaning? Has education *real* purposes?—apart that is from particular purposes of part-icular educators. Will any arguments constitute a justification for the presence of a subject in the curriculum, or rather con-stitute a universally acceptable justification?

The questions are all philosophical in kind because they are concerned with those areas where we are doubtful regarding what is actually at issue. And, although many people are reluctant to admit it, it is characteristic of educational dis-cussion, as we have already begun to see, that it contains such elements.

It must be noted that it is, in a peculiar sense, unfair to complain that philosophy does not give firm and unequivocal answers. This is because if a firm and unequivocal answer can be given to a question then, ipso facto, it is not a philosophical question.

Historically, the philosopher has traditionally concerned himself with very fundamental questions such as 'what do you mean?' and 'how do you know?'. When, in a particular area, the criteria of meaning and the tests for knowledge have become generally accepted, the area concerned has moved away from philosophy and become accepted as a subject in its own right. Thus mathematics and science are rooted in phil-osophy and so are the modern social sciences. This does not mean that no philosophical questions arise in these areas. Each of them has philosophical issues which are crucial and we shall consider some of them at a later stage. But there are conventions for avoiding these for a good part of the time and procedures for effective engagement in the activity, which presume at least some broad degree of agreement.

What sub-divisions may be made among the elements which are left, the philosophical questions? Problems of categorization are considerable but certain main areas are clearly identifiable. One of these is metaphysics; broadly this is the investigation of the reality behind the appearance of things, of what is ultimate, absolute. The fascinating and intriguing quality of this area is the possibility of denying that there is anything at all to investigate. Some philosophers have maintained that all metaphysical statements are meaningless. But there is no doubt that many pronouncements on education still draw on traditional metaphysical positions. These may be of various kinds. For example it may be argued, or assumed, that all aspects of life on earth are imperfect reflections of certain eternal absolutes against which alone they can be judged. Thus moral actions are to be judged by reference to some concept of perfect goodness and works of art in terms of absolute beauty. It is clear that this type of view raises considerable problems regarding the ways in which the existence of such absolutes could be shown or their nature educed.

Frequently, though not necessarily, metaphysical statements are deduced from, or at least linked with, a religious position. And these are of far-reaching importance for education. How is the truth of this kind of proposition to be demonstrated? Can it be? It is not only the validity of teaching religion in schools which depends upon the kind of answers which we give to these questions, or rather upon the kind of answers which can justifiably be given. Upon the views taken depend attitudes to morality, to authority, to the purposes of life, which are likely deeply to imbue the entire approach of a person to education.

Thus although metaphysical questions as such seem distinct from educational questions, metaphysical assumptions frequantly underline educational positions and are used to justify them.

Another important sub-section of philosophy is epistemology or theory of knowledge. Clearly a great deal of education is taken up with questions of what we can know. The educator, or at least the good educator, is held to be one with a concern for truth. What kinds of things can we know to be true and in what kinds of ways? For example, I may claim to know that hydrogen is an element and that two plus two equals four. But these are very different claims. It is logically possible that hydrogen might not be an element. But what could be meant by asserting that two plus two might not equal four? I know that some children have freckles and I know that no children can be members of the stock exchange. But the kind of thing that I know in each case is quite different. That some children have freckles is a matter of fact and it *might* be false. But that no children can be members of the stock exchange, though a matter of fact, is of a different type, for its truth is due to human agreement—albeit well justified agreement.

If we are to teach children knowledge, and it is difficult indeed to imagine a case for not teaching them knowledge, then it would seem important to understand what different types of knowledge there are and to distinguish different tests of truth. What just happens to be true is very different from what could not possibly be false. And it is vital too to consider the bounds of knowledge. Are matters of knowledge and matters of belief, for example, quite distinct categories? Is belief a kind of inferior brand of knowledge, a product without a guarantee? Are there, on the other hand, clear differences between belief and opinion? And, if so, what are these? Should teachers distinguish knowledge from belief and belief from opinion? Clearly they cannot distinguish them in their teaching if they cannot distinguish them for themselves. There are other quite fascinating questions in this area: can I know something without knowing that I know it?; can one ever say justifiably 'I know what that child is thinking'?; what is it 'to know oneself'?; does it ever make sense to say 'I know what should be done'?

It is worth a reminder at this stage that the philosopher is concerned not with dogmatic answers to questions of this kind but with investigating *what is involved in seeking to answer them*.

A third main area of philosophy is concerned with the whole range of questions of value. Just as some philosophers have wished to dismiss all metaphysical questions as meaningless, so there have been claims that all discussions of value are concerned with nothing more than personal opinion or even that they are simply expressions of emotion. Statements of value may be of many kinds. Commending words such as 'good' are used in a wide range of contexts. Three main areas can be identified however as of basic importance in education. First there are moral questions: certain actions are deemed morally right or wrong, certain qualities morally praiseworthy or reprehensible, certain motives desirable or to be condemned. Second, there are aesthetic questions: objects may be regarded as beautiful, tasteful, sublime, degrading, decadent, structurally 'right' and so on. Values are assigned to moral actions and moral qualities, to aesthetic attributes and to works of art themselves. In both these areas there arise crucial questions of definition, of standards, of criteria, of justification of claims put forward and attitudes adopted. And both areas are central to education. Third, there is the question of how the worthwhileness of anything at all can be established (or, again, *if* it can). Certain things are included in educational provision because they are thought to be worthwhile, others excluded either because they are thought worthless, or harmful, or simply of insufficient value to claim a place.

Again let me illustrate through particular examples. Consider how the following statements, typical of ordinary discussion in education, might be defended: 'children ought to learn to be obedient'; 'children should be taught to be tidy'; 'we should always be honest with children, because they need a good example'; 'children should be introduced to good music at an early stage'; 'stories for children should help them to appreciate good literature'; 'children should be left free to follow their own interests'; 'any subject may be worthwhile if it is taught properly'; 'it is much more worthwhile for a child to learn to read than for him to learn to paint'.

In seeing how they can be defended—or attacked—one sees at least some of the problems of some philosophical questions. But, (and this is the vital point), in so doing one is dealing with crucial educational questions. Further it will have been noted, almost certainly, that in considering how to deal with these questions, there will have arisen again questions of what various terms in them mean. Let us now turn to these questions in more detail.

4. MEANING AND LANGUAGE

Some philosophers have held that questions of a philosophical kind are essentially questions which involve misunderstanding, that they are, perhaps, not genuine questions at all. This is, partly, precisely because they have no agreed answers. Without going so far as to say that they are all based on misunderstanding, we can at least begin by considering how much disputed questions may be disputed because of difficulties arising from the language in which they are expressed.

For normal purposes we tend to assume that there is mutual understanding of the words which we are using. In fact this is frequently a false assumption and it may be helpful to turn my attention away from educational issues briefly and consider examples from other areas. Suppose that two keen soccer enthusiasts are arguing about whether or not Everton are a good team. One is maintaining strongly that they are and the other is engaged, equally strongly, in denying it. It might be supposed that what is quite clear is that they are arguing about a question of fact, about the kind of team that Everton are. I want to suggest that this may well not be the case at all. I do not wish to deny that they *think* that this is what they are arguing about. Nor do I wish to deny that this *may* be what they are arguing about. But it may not be.

Let us suppose that both agree that the team's record in League and Cup matches over recent years constitutes an undeniably high and consistent achievement. One of the disputants may then say: 'of course I grant you that, but I still say that they are not a good team. For me a good team must . . .' and he goes on to state qualities which he regards as necessary for a team to be called good and to deny that Everton possess these. This is the vital point to realize: if the other disputant argues that Everton do possess them, then the argument is about the facts of the case; but if he agrees that Everton do not possess them he may well go on to say 'so what?—they are still a good team'. In this case the argument is now about the application of the word 'good'.

In more technical, though not difficult language, the first man wishes to state that the team's record is in itself a sufficient condition of the term 'good' being applied; the second would probably regard it as a necessary condition but not as sufficient; he would also wish to add as a condition the possession of certain stated qualities.

Actually I over-simplified the position when I stated that if they disagreed about Everton not possessing these qualities then they were disagreeing about facts. Again they may have been. But they may have been disagreeing about the meaning of one of these qualities (just as in the other case they were disagreeing about the meaning of 'good'). An example of this would be if they agreed that a good team was one which was aesthetically pleasing. One, however, might regard aesthetically pleasing as involving, necessarily, high individual ball-playing skill, but the other might wish to regard the term as still applicable if, even without this, there were team movements of great precision. (The reader may perhaps consider whether this is really an argument about what 'aesthetic' *means* or about what *is* aesthetic. If so then philosophizing is really underway!)

Another interesting example arose in discussion with my son, then a ten-year-old, about making kits. I had spoken of the kits with many parts as being 'harder' than those with few. He maintained that they were not. In fact there was no disagreement about the kits and the tasks they imposed at all.

C

His point was that there was no actual skill demanded by the larger ones that was not demanded by the smaller ones. Thus he was right—they were not 'harder'. I was holding that as there were many more pieces much more was demanded in completing them. Thus I was right—they were 'harder'. What has shifted is the meaning of hard, the criteria in accordance with which we use the word. Or as my son put it: 'We started by talking about kits but now we're talking about what "hard" means; you've changed it to philosophy'!

If disputes in areas like these are frequently simply about the usage of a term, then it must be expected that this will be more likely to be the case when the area of discussion is abstract or complex or one of high emotional significance.

This last point is of great importance. We have no difficulty in recognizing that certain words have a positive emotional force, for example good, graceful, lovely, skilful. Others have a negative force—bad, ugly, evil, sinister, worthless. But with many other words we may not notice this element so clearly. For example a particular individual may have held to a particular view for a long period of time. This fact about him may be conveyed by saying that he is stubborn. Or that he is steadfast. The facts are the same. But 'stubborn' is used to denigrate and 'steadfast' to praise. Other words may have a different emotional force to different people, or to the same person in different contexts or on different occasions. For example: ambitious, easy-going, tense, sharp. 'Clever' is usually a 'hurrah word' (a pleasing term used by some philosophers—would that all specialist jargon were so easy to grasp!) but may on occasion be a 'boo word', as when a politician is spoken of as 'clever' with the implication that what he is clever at is better not enquired into. 'Intellectual' is a particularly interesting word in this respect—'boo' or 'hurrah'?

24

Certain words may lose meaning to such a degree that they serve only to arouse emotion but normally, one tends to believe, a word has a meaning and we tend also to hold, a clear meaning. Thus the common-sense view is that every word has a meaning which is simply that to which the word refers. The world is made up, it may be thought, of a number of objects which are labelled by us with words which 'stand for' them. It will be recognized that there are more complex problems, in the case of abstract nouns and verbs for example, but fundamentally the labelling view is the common-sense position.

If we are to look more carefully at educational discourse this view requires a considerable examination. It would seem to imply that in order to be able to use a word we have to know what it means and that knowing what it means involves knowing those things to which properly it refers. Consider a word like 'tree'. When is a tree not a tree? This is not intended as a child's riddle, although one has heard it with 'when it is a shoe tree' as an answer. This makes its point however. Clearly a word can have more than one meaning. But what are we to make of 'a rose tree' in this context? Clearly this is the same meaning as the normal one to an extent and yet it also seems distinct.

Do we have to be able to define a word in order to know what it means? Can we *define* tree in such a way that we include not only oak trees, chestnut trees, beech trees and birch trees but rose trees, and yet do not include bushes and shrubs? May we not be driven into saying that trees are what we call trees, puzzled though we may be about how we call them trees *correctly* if we do not know exactly what a tree is.

Or consider what a game is (this example was developed by the philosopher Wittgenstein). What is a game? 'Game' is a common word which is widely used and widely understood.

It is not part of a difficult specialized vocabulary. It is not even confined to adult vocabulary. It is a common word with young children. But what is a game? I suggest that it is interesting to see whether you can define a game, list its necessary characteristics, in such a way as to include everything which you regard as a game and exclude everything which you do not regard as a game. Here are a few specific points. If a child is being tickled it may well be 'having a game with Daddy'. Football is a game; it is also a sport. Motor racing is a sport; is it a game? If not, why not? Chess is a game. So is postman's knock. 'Games' can appear on a school time-table but is there an expectation that *any* game might be played in this period?

In trying to frame a definition of a word like this, it will be noted that there are individual instances which will be unclear in the application of the term to them. It may well seem better to regard some words as having a range of connected meanings rather than as having *a* meaning. Or, in Wittgenstein's phrase, a word may link together meanings which have a 'family resemblance'. For him, the meaning of a word *is* the uses to which we put it in communicating intelligibly.

It is not easy to hold to this view of meaning. We are so used to assuming that a word has a 'proper' or a 'real' meaning that we find ourselves unable fully to grasp the relativity of meaning to use. The view that the meaning of a word is its use does not of course entail Humpty Dumpty's view that a word can be used to mean anything that one likes. It can only be used to mean what it means—if, that is, we wish to communicate. But many words extend and contract in meaning with use and, further, we can recommend usage. The meaning is not fixed, immutable or context-free.

At this stage the best way to proceed is to return to educational discourse and to consider in some detail a word which is central to much discussion of the education of young children, the word 'play'. I shall take this both as an example of my general points about language and as a topic of importance in itself.

5. PLAY AND NATURAL DEVELOPMENT

Let us look first at some common uses of the word 'play' in educational contexts. Here is a fairly random list:—

    A. The children are learning through their play
    B. All they seem to do is to play
    C. All work and no play makes Jack a dull boy
    D. They have a playtime in mid-morning
    E. Play is natural to a child

'A' would seem to be typical of a defence of a certain kind of activity, perhaps in an infants' classroom and perhaps also spoken by the teacher. Play is not necessarily to be regarded here as bad in itself but nevertheless it may be justified as a means to an end, the learning of the child. The assumption seems to be that the children are at school in order to learn and that play is a means of achieving this end. This might not be the context at all however. It could be spoken about a situation in which the play was justified for its own sake; a 'natural', 'free' play situation. But the comment is made that through this play learning is taking place, as a kind of bonus to the enjoyment of the play.

In this case it is interesting to consider where intention lies. Whether it is a situation in a school or what I have called a 'natural' play situation, the child's intention is to play. But in the school setting a teacher is intending that the children should learn. And in the home situation the parents (let us assume) are intending that the children should play but notic-

28

ing that they are learning. Of course, this may not be so; the parents may have 'structured' the play in order that the children should learn. But, I repeat, the children are clearly not intending to learn; they are playing.

Playing in this context then seems to be the activity which the child engages in for its own sake. How does this connect with example 'E'? 'E' seems to be an exceedingly simple statement. But as it stands it is ambiguous. It may mean that being 'natural to a child' is *one* of the characteristics of play—or rather of a child's play. Or it may mean that it is *the* defining characteristic; that the naturalness is what makes it play. From our consideration of 'A' it seemed that we wanted to regard play as the natural activity which the child engaged in for its own sake. But do we want to say that all such activity is play? Is the child's 'natural' feeding play? We might perhaps want to say, remembering intention, that to the child it is. But it does not seem certain that we would wish to say this.

We may be helped by looking at example 'B'. Here it seems that play has 'boo' undertones. The implication is that something else ought to be going on. The children only seem to be playing when in fact they ought to be . . . 'learning'? 'working'? It might be thought to be a reply to the accusation that the children seem only to be playing to answer with 'A'. To many doubtless it would be; the end (learning) would be thought to justify the means (playing). And as the means is some kind of natural activity which, presumably, the children find pleasurable, this might be thought to count in its favour. But some might doubt this, arguing that even though the children are learning through their play, nevertheless they ought to be working.

We thus come across the word which, in ordinary parlance, seems to be the opposite of play. Clearly it is an opposition which is implied in 'C', with an implied suggestion that play is a necessary element in childhood, and in 'D', where play is seen as a break from the 'real' activity of a school—'work'?

Play thus seems to have the idea of an activity which is engaged in for its own sake and of something which is not work. But 'work' too has more than one idea associated with it. At times it carries with it the association of something done for the sake of something else rather than for its own sake, of something instrumental rather than something of intrinsic value. But it need not mean this. We can certainly talk of work for its own sake and, in this sense, it seems odd to contrast work with play. Sometimes the main association of work may be thought to be effort, the expenditure of energy. But play, in this sense, can certainly be hard work. Sometimes we refer to children working hard at their play.

We may perhaps think of work as serious and, in this sense, as contrasting with play. But certainly children can be said frequently to take their play seriously. And, looked at from the adult standpoint, it may have a serious function, as in example 'A'.

What may be concluded from this brief discussion about the role of play in education? First, as a preliminary, it has been noted that play and work are not simple concepts which exclusively and exhaustively characterize the activities of education. Second, it must be realized that the philosopher has no wish to lay down a personal view of what ought to be happening in education. We may all have different ends which we value and which we should like the educational process to serve. But it can be shown, for example, that if learning is taken as the end (though we shall have to ask later about what is learned), and if learning can be achieved through play, then play serves an educational end. Suppose that someone were to deny that learning took place through play. In order to sustain their case they would have to show that, as a matter of fact, children did not learn while playing. But what we have seen is that, to show this, they have not only to demonstrate what as a matter of fact does or does not happen in a wide range of situations, but use an acceptable definition of play. We have seen also, however, that there is no one single definition.

We have to beware here of a common move, that of creating an argument which appears to give us information about matters of fact but actually only says how a certain person intends to use a word. That children cannot learn through play, which would normally be said to be false as a matter of fact, might be made *necessarily* true as a matter of definition. What would happen would be that the person who was arguing the case would not allow to count as play anything in the course of which learning took place. This is not as wholly unlikely or as implausible as it may seem when stated here in a context where there is a heightened awareness of language. The person arguing the case might maintain: 'Granted there are certain activities which look like play, in the course of which children learn, but, just because of this, it is obvious that they are not mere play. Play, in its essence, has no purpose beyond itself and thus if learning occurs it is not really play'. It looks plausible now perhaps. But we can deal with it. A word has no essence. It has uses. And normally we do not use 'play' in this restricted sense. Of course we might do so. And if we were to do so then children could not learn through play. But this would have told us nothing new about children; it would not have altered the facts; indeed it would not tell us anything about children at all. It would simply tell us something about the way in which the word play was to be used.

The view that a word means what it is used to mean does pose problems. It may begin to suggest that we have no control over the word at all. Frequently we are to some extent aware of this in our ordinary conversation. We use phrases such as: '. . . well, I don't quite mean that when I say . . . what I mean is . . .'; 'I'm not using the word in quite that sense; 'I've never thought of . . . as implying that . . .'; 'it doesn't really mean that to me'; 'When I say . . . I feel that it isn't quite the word but I'm not sure what other word I can use'.

We are aware of ranges of meaning and of shades of meaning. And, as in the case of the man who took play to mean an activity in which no learning takes place, or as in the case above 'When I say . . . what I mean is . . .', we may stipulate a definition. Stipulative definitions are exceedingly important if we are to make sense of educational discussion and it is worth looking at them closely.

The oddity about defining play as an activity which involves no learning, or at least stipulating that this is one of the defining characteristics of play, is that this does not seem to be a usual condition of calling something play at all. But we may well find it necessary to stipulate a definition of a word for the purposes of a particular argument, without postulating that the word 'means that' in every usage and regardless of context.

For example, taking 'play' again, I may wish to construct an argument referring repeatedly to those activities which young children will engage in spontaneously for the pleasure inherent in them. Then I may say that I shall use the word 'play' to refer to these activities. In so doing I may recognize perfectly well both that it is arguable whether there are activities of this kind that are not play and whether there are senses of play which do not involve these activities. I merely say that 'for the purpose of argument I shall use this definition'. In so doing I am making myself clearer.

The problem is that while the reader of an argument of this

kind may note the proviso, the caution, as he begins to read, it may more and more be forgotten as time goes on. So that ultimately, having decided that the argument is valid, he may say—'It has been shown that through play . . .' without realizing that the conclusions are limited to play in the sense in which it was defined. The unscrupulous purveyor of educational advice may well *play* upon this. Taking a stipulative definition of his key word before he begins, a definition suiting his own case, he gradually 'forgets' this as the argument proceeds and emerges with conclusions as though they were applicable to a different, or perhaps a wider definition. We shall see other examples of this later.

This is not to say—I must repeat this—that there is anything wrong in itself with stipulative definition. Frequently it is necessary. The very fuzziness of words forces it as a means of producing clarity. But the clarity is bought at the expense of narrowing usage and this has always to be remembered.

Let us consider another word which is central to much educational discussion and which often appears in close association with 'play'. This is 'natural'. I used it myself in example 'E' earlier: 'Play is natural to a child'. What does this mean? By this stage there may be a number of points which you, the reader, feel able to make about the word 'natural'. You may wish to consider it yourself in various contexts and from various aspects before going on to read my discussion of it.

The first point that I find it necessary to make is that 'natural' is a hurrah word. When we talk of something as natural we are normally, I think, not only describing it but in some way commending it. This may not always have been so and that it is now (*if* it is) may reflect certain dominant values in our society. That it is a commending word is not, of course, a philosophical point. It is a point of fact; what philosophers call an empirical point. That is to say that the way to test whether or not it is true is not to consider the nature of 'natural' as a concept but to see how people actually use the word. So you may judge that I am just wrong in thinking it a commending word. Prima facie however I think that I could make out a good case. Certainly it seems to me that, 'unnatural' is normally used to condemn as well as to describe. For example it is a quite usual argument against circuses that the animals are required to do things which are unnatural for them, as though this in itself *is* an argument against the activity. A defence against this might be either to argue that the activity was not unnatural, or, alternatively, to accept that it was unnatural but to deny the pejorative implication of the term, to say that 'unnatural' did not entail 'undesirable'.

Descriptively, what is meant by designating an activity as natural to a child? One reply might be that it is anything which a child does instinctively, as a direct outcome of its own organic nature. But, as a matter of fact it is not at all clear what is meant, in human terms, by behaviour of this kind. The developing child grows in a context of constant interaction with others in society. There are no detailed patterns of behaviour which just unfold. Talk of instincts, in human beings, soon becomes talk of the most generalized motivating factors, hunger, sex, self-preservation, curiosity—factors which are so wide as to be almost empty of clear meaning. Certainly we cannot equate 'natural for a child' with 'what a child would do left to itself' for it would do virtually nothing. Children are cuddled, stimulated, spoken to, put to bed, woken up and so on and so on. We treat them in various ways. So how can one begin to distinguish what is organically natural from their response to varying kinds of treatment?

Why then should natural activity be commended? It would seem that beliefs about freedom—another word to be examined more closely later—lead us to feel or think or believe (which is

34

the appropriate term?) that we should not impose ourselves on the child. But there is a sense in which the human being is unnatural. Communication between human beings is by means of speech, fundamentally, and this capacity for speech has evolved gradually over exceedingly long periods of time. Yet no one in fact is so absurd as to suppose that the natural thing to do is to let a child 'discover' language for itself. It is encouraged to learn from the social context in which it is brought up. An English child 'naturally' learns to speak English and a French child to speak French. Yet in this natural learning of its own language, it is necessarily learning a mass of arbitrary symbols and conventional associations.

Is it in any way 'natural' for a child to be moral? Rousseau, in the eighteenth century, maintained that the child was naturally good. He has his followers today. But is 'good' a natural concept at all? Would it not be better to say that the child naturally just *is*? Psychological evidence suggests that he is necessarily egocentric for a long period; that he is simply incapable of seeing the world objectively; that he has gradually to learn to distinguish himself as an object within a world of objects. How then could he be naturally good? (or, for that matter, naturally evil or wicked or sinful?) He has to learn the differences between the effects of various kinds of behaviour and, until he does this, the language of morality simply does not apply to him at all. But how would it make sense to leave him to learn these differences naturally?

I am suggesting therefore that claims to defend particular educational practices by designating them as natural need very close examination. This may be argued even more strongly when, instead of using the adjective natural, the argument involves a claim 'that human nature shows us that we should ...' At times, we may even read 'that Human Nature ...' —the capital letters being used to personify Human Nature as some kind of authority. By now it should be clear that such claims are largely empty. Empirical evidence—largely from anthropology—in fact suggests that there is little if anything which can be regarded as universally true of human nature. Homo sapiens may be a biological species but a human being is largely a social product.

Thus appeals to play as natural do not really get us very far. Nor do references to allowing the child to grow naturally. The metaphor of growth arose largely to counter that of moulding. The child as a plant replaced the child as clay. Again we must note that some of the issues here are empirical; how far the human organism *can* be moulded and what *does* just grow if left alone is a matter of fact— difficult though it may be to find out. Other aspects of the question are evaluative; we may differ very much in the extent to which we think it right or justifiable to attempt to 'mould' human beings. But parts of the question can be answered by examining the language itself. What would it be to allow the child to grow naturally? If a plant grows naturally it becomes the 'mature adult' which is determined by the interaction of the genetic potential within its seed with the nourishment from the soil, the warmth of the sun, the moisture it receives and so on. No amount of clever gardening could turn dahlias into rhododendrons. And when gardeners, or horticulturalists, develop a new type of rose, thus using their limited ability to produce change, they make decisions as to what is desirable and plan accordingly.

It is exceedingly unclear what could be meant by allowing a child to grow naturally. What are the equivalents of the manure and the moisture and the sun? The essential part about a child is that he becomes an adult through inter-action with other human beings in a social environment. He cannot be (and I mean *cannot be* not *is not* or *should not be*) left just

36

to grow with the addition of food and warmth, if he is to develop into a person. Even a decision not to decide what kind of child we want to produce, paradoxically, *is* a decision to produce a certain kind of child; one, for example, who is not docile, imitative and over-dependent on adult models.

By looking at certain aspects of the words 'play', 'natural', and 'growth' we have uncovered a number of difficulties which lie in educational theories which rely upon these terms. And we have done so through an examination of the terms themselves. This does not mean however that we have been merely playing with words nor does it mean that we have destroyed the theories which use the terms.

Let me take these two points one at a time. First, we have not just been playing with words. The words are the vehicles of the concepts in which our thinking is embodied. If they refer to a range of rather unclear concepts then, in using them, we are in danger of confusing ourselves and of failing to communicate. These dangers can only be reduced by examination of our language; by asking how the key words are used, by stipulating our definitions where necessary, by ensuring that the conclusions of an argument are not extended by enlarging the definitions of terms en route.

Second, we are not destroying an argument by questioning the language in which it is expressed, though we may be forcing a re-formulation of the argument. Thus personally I hold strongly that those who advocate the natural growth of the child against those who hold moulding theories are usually on the side which I would myself support, though with many provisos. But I do not think that the case can be sustained by appeal to 'natural growth' as such, for reasons which I have outlined. In fact these advocates wish for a greater degree of individual freedom; and so, very frequently, do I.

I am not arguing at any point in this book that all

educational arguments will evaporate if only we will look carefully at our language in expressing them. I am urging however, that, unless we do this, we shall not know what we are arguing about or, indeed, whether we are arguing about any point of substance at all, for we *may* not be.

One element which theories concerning play and natural growth have in common is that they have produced a shift in our concept of the teacher. By stressing activities and processes which take place without deliberate and intentional adult participation (interference?) they have rendered questionable the necessity of the teacher as a part of the educational process, at least at some of its stages.

It thus seems vital that we should examine the concept of 'teaching' and that of 'teacher' to see what these involve. In doing so it is necessary to try to rid ourselves of masses of existing presuppositions. One of the problems of thinking philosophically is that our pre-existing patterns of thought, expectations and associations have a nasty habit of trickling back in, however hard we try to keep them out. Play, natural, growth, teaching, teacher—all these are terms which are rich in associations for us and these associations become part of the meaning of the words for us. This is accepted. Indeed I have stressed it. Yet we must attempt to put these on one side for the purposes of certain arguments, if only because our associations may be radically different from those of others with whom we are endeavouring to communicate. Later we must let them back in; *must* necessarily do so. They are part and parcel of the terms. But for particular purposes they must be kept out. In this case the purpose is to see what seems to be characteristic of the terms 'teacher' and 'teaching' in normal usage, for however much we may hold that it is use which gives meaning to a word, without some measure of agreement on 'proper use' we could not communicate at all.

6. TEACHING AND THE TEACHER

In considering teaching and the teacher it might be thought that we are simply considering one topic in two aspects; teaching is the activity in which the teacher is engaged and, as the activity cannot take place on its own, teaching presupposes a teacher and the existence of a teacher implies the activity of teaching. Such a simple analysis, however, itself involves problems. Nor are they merely verbal problems. A failure to take the matter further can lead to practical mistakes. We shall consider first the activity of teaching and then the role of a teacher and, in so doing, we shall see why differences of emphasis occur.

What is going on if someone is teaching? It is clear that no particular place is required for the activity nor is any particular professional qualification. The greater part of the teaching of young children is undertaken by their parents. Before 'teachers' receive the average child, he or she has learned a wide range of skills, habits and knowledge. The complex business of speech has been fundamentally mastered by the normal five-year-old, though, of course, there is great development still ahead. In ordinary parlance we speak not only of parents teaching their children to walk but of birds teaching their young to fly. In this sense what seems basically to be involved in teaching is the intention to secure learning on the part of those taught.

To say this, is not to say that learning necessitates teaching. When I referred to the skills, habits and knowledge acquired

39

by young children I did not wish to imply that all these had been consciously and deliberately taught. Much would seem just to be picked up. Again referring to our ordinary usage, it is quite common for people to say 'life taught me that . . .'. Though 'life' is being personified in this expression, it is clearly only a figurative way of saying 'I have learned from the experiences of life that . . .'. (Incidentally, though, one may note the danger of figurative expression, which, misleadingly, suggests the passivity of the learner and the embodiment of authority in the experiences of life.)

So to say that learning is taking place is not necessarily to say that teaching is taking place. In this respect the word learning does not stand to teaching as does buying to selling. One can learn without a teacher but cannot buy without a seller.

Can one, reversing the situation, teach without learning taking place? Can I say that I have been teaching my son to swim but that he has not learned to swim? It seems obvious that I can. Yet, in another sense, teaching does presuppose learning, for the purpose of the activity is to secure learning. It is best in this sense to consider that 'teach' has the dual aspect of intention and success or, as others have put it, task and achievement. To teach is to set about the task of producing learning, though whether one successfully achieves one's aim remains an open question.

One might ask whether there are any particular activities which constitute teaching. To consider this further I will take the discussion into the context of the school. Let us suppose that a Headmaster asks a child to go along to Miss Smith's room and see if she is teaching; the child returns and reports that she isn't teaching, the class are working on their own and she is walking round and helping them individually. This may be a perfectly proper reply in context. The child may have known that the Headmaster wanted to know whether he could interrupt Miss Smith to give her a message. When he asked whether she was teaching he wanted to know whether she was engaged in an activity centred upon herself and having —or expecting!—the class's unified attention. And the child knew from the context what was meant. It is clear that if the Headmaster had subsequently criticized Miss Smith for not having been teaching he would have been acting absurdly.

We can see that if the child had been a sophisticated embryonic philosopher, with a philosopher's awkward-mindedness, other replies would have been possible. Suppose that the child had returned and said 'the children were learning and so Miss Smith was teaching'. Or suppose, in different circumstances, he had reported that Miss Smith was talking to the class and they appeared to be listening but he couldn't say whether Miss Smith was teaching.

This deliberately artificial example reveals certain points about the nature of teaching. First it emphasises that teaching can often be defined in terms of the intention of producing learning. There is thus no need to regard it as a necessary condition of teaching that any talking, any telling, any instruction should be going on, although it was a necessary condition in the context in which the Headmaster wished to know whether Miss Smith could be interrupted.

The problem with the reply that the children were learning and so Miss Smith was teaching is two-fold. First, as we saw earlier, the learning might have been going on quite incidentally, regardless of, or even in spite of Miss Smith's efforts. The children might even have been learning that it was not very profitable to listen to Miss Smith! Second, there is no way in which the child could have observed the learning itself taking place; it would have had to have been an inference from what was observed and might have been mistaken. Learning and teaching are alike in that no one activity characterizes them.

In the case in which the child reported that Miss Smith was talking to the class but he could not say whether they were learning and thus whether she was teaching, 'teaching' is of course being used in its 'success' sense. But, we must note, the talking to the class did not itself guarantee teaching in the intention sense. She might just have been talking about something with no intention of producing learning at all.

Take an imaginary walk down a school corridor. Mr. Jones is drawing diagrams on the blackboard; Mrs. Wright is talking rapidly with much gesturing; Mr. Carter is playing the piano; Mr. Paterson is standing on his head; Miss Robertson is sharpening a pencil; Miss Anderson is putting a plaster on a child's finger; Mr. Green is reading aloud from a book; Mrs. Harris is marking a child's sums. Are they teaching? Mr. Jones' diagrams may clearly be intended to teach the intricacies of a Euclidean theorem. But they might be instructions to help the football team reach the ground for Saturday's match. If the latter, is he teaching? He certainly intends that they should learn how to get there. So is this teaching? Mrs. Wright may well be teaching but she may be giving a pupil a severe reprimand. Is this teaching? She might describe it as 'teaching him a lesson'. Mr. Carter may be accompanying class singing. Is this teaching? He may be entertaining the class to his version of the latest pop hit as a reward for their earlier good behaviour. Is this teaching?—teaching them that good behaviour pays? Mr. Paterson may be giving a demonstration in a gym lesson or showing that he can still stand on his head to a sceptical class who think that at his age this is impossible. And so on.

What is clear is that the various activities may all be perfectly proper for a teacher to indulge in though we may be unclear whether or not we wish to call them teaching, because of our uncertainties about the criteria to apply for the proper use of this term.

Partly this is because of doubts about the word 'learning'. Children may be learning something quite other than that which the teacher intends to teach them. They may even be 'learning' something which is wrong because of a slip of the tongue or a failure to explain clearly or a moment's inattention or the ignorance of the teacher. We can learn habits, skills, facts, attitudes. We can learn briefly or for life. We can re-learn that which we have forgotten.

Other difficulties arise because of distinctions between 'teacher' and 'teaching' which I referred to earlier. If, basically, teaching is concerned with producing learning then, as I have indicated, no one activity or set of activities is demanded by the term. For many people, however, the concept of teaching involves talking, telling, instructing. This is largely perhaps because of their own experience of being taught. But its practical consequences are important. Too often, I suggest, the teacher feels that he must 'teach', in this sense, in order to be fulfilling his function properly. If I am right in this, then the failure to think sufficiently clearly about the nature of a term may be leading to a wealth of worthy but inappropriate activity. That is, its adverse practical consequences are severe.

Many teachers however, particularly teachers of young children, have now realized that however we may use the word 'teach', the purpose of their task as teachers, or of part of it at least, is to produce learning, and that the methods they adopt may or may not involve a great deal of talking. Whether they involve this or not is to be judged by the varying degrees of effectiveness of the various methods in securing their purposes.

43

Ironically, such has been the swing of opinion and judgment in this respect that it has now come to be held by some extremists not only that talking is not a necessary condition of teaching but almost that it is a vice in a teacher! Teachers are spoken of as 'creators of learning situations'. My suggestion is that the test of the teaching lies in its results rather than in the nature of the activity at all.

But why should one assume that a teacher must necessarily be teaching? Of course the word 'teacher' implies a close connection with the activity of teaching. But we must remember that to call someone a teacher is to refer to a social role which he or she performs. Not all those who are professionally engaged in teaching are referred to as teachers. For example driving instructors are teaching pupils to drive, football coaches are teaching their teams new tactics, store managers will teach their new staff the procedures of the store, policemen may well actually come into schools to teach road safety. A teacher however is one who operates within society to initiate its children and young people into a wide range of skills and knowledge, habits and activities, procedures and possibilities, problems and interests, and to further their pursuit of these. In so doing the teacher may quite properly do many other things than teach, certainly he will if we take this word in a limited sense. In poor areas particularly it may be exceedingly difficult to distinguish the teacher from the social worker. Before he can teach, the teacher may have to set about creating the kind of conditions in which learning may take place.

In all situations however there are a number of tasks, proper to a teacher, which are not 'teaching'. One may mention keeping records of pupils' progress; writing reports; preparing lessons; supervizing outings; refereeing matches; assessing work; listening to pupils' personal problems; checking stock and tidying cupboards. Though teaching and learning may be thought central to a school's activities they are not all that goes on there.

It is helpful, I think, to consider the role of the teacher by comparison with and contrast to other jobs and professions. The point which requires stress is consideration of the purposes which are being fulfilled by the job.

In a chocolate factory an employee is working by an automatic wrapping machine. As the bars come out wrapped by the machine, she has to remove any which are imperfectly wrapped. Even here there are possible elements of doubt over exactly what she must do. Are there minor imperfections which she may let pass? If there are, can one lay down the exact conditions which have to exist before she acts to remove a bar? Or, in philosophical terms, what are the criteria for regarding a block as satisfactorily packed, in the absence of one of which the employee acts?

A roadsweeper is working his way along a tree-lined street in autumn. His job is difficult for the very obvious reason that as he sweeps up the leaves more come down. But there is little, if any, difficulty in determining what he is trying to do; there would seem to exist only marginal difficulties of deciding where public property ends and private property begins or whether it is his job to sweep up broken glass on a pavement or to leave it to the milkman who dropped the bottle. There may be a range of difficulties over methods, over how he can successfully sweep the street with a maximum result for a minimum effort, but these are distinct from difficulties of aim or purpose.

The reader may care to examine other jobs from this point of view but I shall take something of a jump in the type of occupation (judged by social esteem anyway) and consider the task of defending counsel in a legal action. In this case his role within the system can be summarized as that of securing the acquittal of the defendant. But there is a range of questions which can be asked about this purpose besides those of technical effectiveness, that is of the effectiveness of the technique for securing this purpose. For example is he justified in casting doubt upon the general character of prosecution witnesses? To do so might secure acquittal but the question of whether the procedure is justified is not answered by this alone. Or is he justified in appealing to the emotions of the jury in the hope that these will override their rationality? Again the procedure may 'work' but this alone does not show that it is justified.

Consider the vocation of the doctor. At times his problems again appear to be technical, to be problems of securing an agreed purpose by discovering the right techniques to do so. A patient has a broken leg; the doctor has to set the bone so that it will heal properly as soon as possible. A child has a high temperature and is feverish; the doctor has to diagnose what is causing the symptoms and to prescribe treatment which will lessen the child's pain, check the infection and restore normal health as soon as possible.

Even in these apparently simple cases however there are problems which are not those of technique alone. Suppose that one method of setting takes much longer but is rather more likely to be fully effective; does this in itself answer the question of which method to use? Or suppose that the most effective cure for the child involves further pain of quite an acute kind for a short period. What are the criteria? And who decides? And would the decision be different if the patient were an adult? And, if so, why?

If such arguments can arise with these examples, it needs no elaboration to indicate that similar problems arise much more acutely with questions such as the suffering of those who are incurably ill, transplant of organs, and the treatment of the mentally ill.

My suggestion regarding the role of the teacher is that he is in a position where many of his problems are not technical at all. By this I mean that he has to make decisions about ends as well as about means. In order to make my meaning totally clear here let me return to my use of the word 'technical'. In the sense in which I use it here, it has nothing to do with machinery and the mechanical. It means simply 'concerned with technique', with the best means of reaching certain agreed ends.

When I claim that the teacher's problems extend far beyond those of technique I am not making a conceptual claim but an empirical one; in other words, it does not follow *necessarily* from the fact that someone is a teacher that his concerns extend beyond the technical. For example a teacher might be hired for particular teaching purposes and told by his employer that it was not for him to question what he was being told to do; it was for him to get on and do it. The 'end state' of the teaching process being laid down externally, the sole problem for the teacher is the efficacy of the various means of producing it. This, however, is an exceptional case. Even in countries where the content of the curriculum is laid down centrally and where there is a high degree of consensus on basic values and a high degree of enforcement of the agreed line, there will be a number of broader questions for the teacher to answer.

It will be recalled that in my discussion of what might be meant by the best method of teaching reading I showed that there could be considerable doubt about the exact nature of the end state (the child who 'can read') and about the side effects of various methods; the teacher has to judge in these areas.

In many societies however the teacher is given much more scope than this; it is for him to decide not only how various things should be taught but what should be taught. There are of course certain limits on this freedom and a number of pressures are exerted upon the teacher, but much freedom remains. Let me illustrate the point in the British context.

Primary school teachers face a number of expectations from parents and from society at large. Children *are* expected to learn to read. This is simply a fact. But a great deal of what goes on in primary schools is determined by the teachers. The substitution of many modern methods in mathematics is partly misunderstood if it is regarded simply as a change of methods. The 'new mathematics' is concerned not just, or even primarily with new methods of reaching the old ends but with new ends. There has been a judgement on the part of the proponents of change in this area that understanding of the underlying nature of mathematics is more important than the ability to compute rapidly through rote learning.

In secondary schools there are massive pressures to comply with the demands of higher and further education and of employers, frequently mediated through the public examination system. But there are still great freedoms in choice of subjects and of syllabus within subjects.

At a later point I shall discuss what *rights* teachers have to make decisions in this area. My point at the moment is simply that, in fact, they do make such decisions and thus that a teacher is one who does more than teach; crucially he decides, to a considerable extent, what he should teach.

We have seen also that there is another sense in which teachers, in their social role, are not simply those who teach. They are those who carry through the work of those institutions, schools, colleges and so on, which are established within society to be the means of initiation of its young. And in so doing there is a wide range of activities, administrative activities for example, which cannot be called teaching but which are demanded by the professional role of the teacher.

Thus if a teacher were to carry through a careful analysis of what was involved in the concept of teaching—and I have given some basic guidelines for this earlier in the chapter—he would gain only part of the map of his task as a teacher. For the rest he would have to consider the nature of society as a whole and the relationship of his role to the wider patterns of social concern.

7. THE CURRICULUM

If children cannot just be left to grow naturally then not only do they require teachers but decisions have to be made about what should be taught. It may be noticed that in saying this I suggest already that no clear-cut view is possible regarding what should be taught, for if one could say without any question of doubt what should be taught then there is nothing to *decide*; the question becomes simply one of implementation. By this point however, it will have become clear that there is little in education that can be stated without question of doubt!

To say that there will remain doubts and uncertainties is not however to say that all is mere opinion, let alone that rational discussion is powerless. So let us consider the kinds of argument that might be put forward in justification of the teaching of any given subject or area or topic or activity (or ... ?—I am deliberately trying not to prejudge part of the issue through the choice of any one word here.).

Broadly, it can be said that justificatory arguments fall into two categories, the instrumental and the intrinsic. The basic logical point here is a simple one but a crucial one. To justify something instrumentally is to justify it as a means to something else. Clearly such an argument has three conditions: (i) one has to show that it is a means to the end; (ii) one has to show that it is the best means to the end; (iii) one has to show the desirability of the end. Following (iii) one can see that any instrumental argument presupposes the justification of something else, the postulated end, on intrinsic grounds. If asked for the reason for something, one cannot go on ad infinitum justifying in terms of something else. If A is justified as a means to B and B as a means to C and C as a means to D, at some point something has to be justified for its own sake.

This can be illustrated from one's experience of a stage in the development of many young children when the question "why?" is predominant in their vocabulary:

'Can John come out to play?'

'I am afraid not; he is watching television.'

'Why?'

'He is interested in trains and the programme is about trains.'

'Why?'

'Well it just is about trains. And I suppose he's interested in them because his Daddy is.'

'Why is his Daddy interested in them?'

And so on! At some stage the activity has to be defended in its own terms.

Much in education, however, is customarily defended in instrumental terms. The acquisition of many skills is regarded as necessary—'because they will be needed later on'. Thus the teaching of reading might be defended on the grounds that the adult in our society needs to be able to read. Historically there have been times when the teaching of reading was defended by the argument that it would enable the pupil to read the Bible. The reading itself was merely a means to an end. In a sense the defence of reading is always likely to be instrumental; there seems to be no intrinsic worthwhileness in casting one's eye rapidly over a series of arbitrary symbols. But there can be considerable differences in the way in which the instrumental task is interpreted. Reading material may be chosen which is suited to the development of the skill of reading but which has no intrinsic value itself at all, or certainly none which is recognizable by the child. On the other hand great emphasis may be placed on the value of the material which is being read and the child led to the mastery of the instrumental process through a stress upon the intrinsic.

The promise of future delights is frequently held out as intended encouragement to the completion of instrumental activities held to be boring in themselves. Generations of children were driven through the intricacies of Latin grammar as a means to the alleged delights of Ovid and Virgil. 'Unless you can . . . you will not be able to . . .' is a frequent form of argument. To many the string of instrumental connections must seem endless and the intrinsic pleasure never forthcoming.

One main area of instrumental argument is that of vocational education. This is not to say that nothing of intrinsic value goes on in this area. But, by its very nature, vocational education is concerned with a future state, adult employment, and with the educational process as a means to this.

Some people would tend to decry all educational processes which are not intrinsically worthwhile. Again one conceptual move may be noted. It is possible to define 'educational', stipulatively, in such a way that intrinsic worthwhileness is built into the term as a necessary condition of its use. Then, it may be argued, nothing which is not intrinsically worthwhile is educational. But this says nothing beyond the question of how the word is being used. To make it more plausible, the argument sometimes takes the form of saying that only the intrinsically worthwhile is *genuinely* educational, implying that all else is quasi-educational or pseudo-educational. It is difficult, however, to see how an argument for nothing but that which is intrinsically worthwhile to be in the curriculum could be maintained, except by dogmatic assertion.

A more acceptable move would seem to be that of arguing that if a given end, the worthwhileness of which is for the moment assumed, can be pursued through means which involve intrinsically worthwhile elements themselves, then, other things being equal, these are to be preferred to means which seem to have no value beyond their instrumental efficiency.

It is clear, however, that these arguments seem secondary to those which arise in pursuit of intrinsic justification. The *real* problem, it may be argued, is that of showing that any activity is intrinsically more worthwhile than any other. Presumably certain choices have to be made concerning the activities which are to be pursued in schools, the areas which are to be studied, the skills which are to be developed, the range of interests which is to be encouraged. As we have seen, instrumental justifications serve only to push the justification problem back a stage. How can we show that there are intrinsic studies which are of greater value or more worth pursuing than others?

Attempts to show intrinsic worthwhileness frequently turn out to be disguised instrumental arguments. Activity A is defended because it contains element B, but then it is a means to B and thus B needs justifying. For example compulsory games may be defended because they involve team spirit, but one may then ask why develop team spirit? (one could also, of course, question whether it is a *fact* that team spirit is thus developed).

The oddity about defending anything *in its own terms* is that the defence either refers to something else, and can thus be characterized as disguised instrumentalism, or appears to be mere assertion. (Why does one say 'mere'?). Suppose that I wish to defend the introduction of a particular class of children to the music of Bach. I could say that this music contained various worthwhile elements, but would then have to defend the worthwhileness of the elements. At some point, I suggest, one has just to assert. Even if I were to say that this music can give great enjoyment or is of great beauty, I could be asked to defend enjoyment or beauty as ends. At some stage one has to say 'enough, no more'. And to do so is not a sign of weakness but a logical necessity. To be rational is to give reasons. But a train of reasons must stop somewhere. And it stops with an assertion.

This may not mean that the assertion is itself wholly arbitrary. Some would wish to maintain this. The extreme view is that nothing can be shown to be more worthwhile than anything else. Others would hold that there are agreed standards of worthwhileness which can be applied even if they remain open always logically to doubt—after all, so do the theories of science remain open. Another possible line of defence is to suggest that though *ultimate* worthwhileness may never be demonstrable, *educational* worthwhileness can be shown.

The argument here is to suggest that certain things are necessarily true of education. That is to say that if these elements were not present the activity concerned would not be called education. Education, it may be argued, is necessarily concerned with learning. Certain activities are much more fruitful than others in their learning potential. Thus to engage in these is educationally more worthwhile. There is, for example, simply more to learn about playing chess than there is about playing bingo. Thus, even if one were to hold that bingo is worthwhile for all who find it worthwhile, one could not hold—it is argued—that it is educationally very worthwhile because once you know how to play you know how to play. The rules tell you all the procedures—which is far from the case in chess.

It must quickly be added that learning potential hardly seems to be the sole criterion of worthwhileness; one might consider it more worthwhile to learn about politics than about chess for example. It could be argued that chess is self-contained. And certainly the world could exist without it. Learning about politics, on the other hand, leads into further learning of history, geography, economics, questions of morality and so forth. Yet this argument might be reversed; it could be held that politics is not worthwhile in itself but is rather a means to producing the kind of society in which worthwhile activities can be pursued—for example the playing of chess!

Another possible line of argument is that broadly there are various ways in which man has come to organize his view of the world and that these are not arbitrary but are imposed by the nature of the situation—although it took a long time for them to be recognized. Education may thus be characterized as the process whereby children are brought to understanding in these areas—areas which we shall consider more fully in the next chapter. Again however one could argue that while doubtless *some* people must be thus initiated it seems very doubtful whether one can argue that *all* people must necessarily be thus initiated. We might wish to offer opportunities of *appreciation* to all but how does appreciation rest upon understanding? What kind of question is this? Is it empirical—that is to say do we answer it by observing people's interests and discerning, as a matter of fact, whether their appreciation increases with their understanding? If it is that kind of question then it is possible that we may get a negative, or partly negative answer. In other words, we must be prepared to find some people with high appreciation and low understanding. Some might then question this, in effect arguing that the question was not an empirical one at all. If a person is *really* to appreciate anything, it may be argued, then he *must* understand it. Thus understanding is made, by definition, a necessary condition of appreciation. In this case, of course, there is no need to carry out an empirical enquiry because the class of

55

those who appreciate x but do not understand x is rendered empty before the enquiry begins—there could not be any such.

Here one would wish, perhaps, to argue about whether such a definition of appreciation (or of 'real appreciation') accords with usage or, if not, whether it could be justified as a stipulation. But it could be disputed, in any case, whether 'appreciation of' or 'understanding of' is the more worthwhile. Which is the educational end? If I understand a work of art but do not appreciate it, what is my understanding worth? Yet I may, by some criteria appreciate it without being taught about it. And may I understand it without being taught about it? The questions go on in a complex criss-cross of inter-relationships.

Such, however, is the nature of philosophical issues. It is this which makes them philosophical. All positions seem open to new challenges. And if at times it seems very confusing—even depressing, for some who think that they like things cut and dried—one may fairly ask whether we should really like it if questions of worthwhileness had indisputable answers. It is sometimes rather casually argued that if things are ultimately matters of opinion they are not worth arguing about. Yet I would reverse this and say that it is matters of fact that are not worth arguing about. If a proposition x is true then it is true; all that remains is to accept its truth. There is nothing to argue about. But opinions are not the same things as whims. An opinion may be more or less rational even if not ultimately 'provable'. Such, I suggest, are opinions about what is worth including in the curriculum.

But who should decide what is actually to be included? There are various candidates in the field. The children?—consumer choice! Their parents? The teachers? Society as a whole? Again note the form of the question—who *should* decide? It is a question of justification, not of fact; it is philosophical not sociological. We are here concerned not with who does decide but with who ought to do so. This might be thought to be just another evaluation. Some will think that the decision should rest with one group, some with another. Cynics might say that in the case of their own children teachers think that they, as parents, should decide but that for everyone else's children it is the teachers who should choose! In a sense it is correct to suggest that the question is an open one but it is not, I think, wholly open. For example we might qualify it by asking 'who should decide in a democratic society?' In this case we accept, tacitly, that other conclusions might be reached, or would be reached, in a totalitarian context, but say that we are concerned with our society. It might then be suggested that, although the question remains open if seen out of context, certain things are necessarily true of a democratic society.

If education is concerned broadly with passing on those elements in a society's culture which are thought to be valuable, then the choice of curriculum activities could not basically be the children's choice. For they lack the grounds for making rational choice. That is why they are being educated. This is not to say, of course, that there can be no element of choice for children. Only that they, as consumers, cannot say fundamentally what is to be made available for them.

If teachers claim the right to decide then there are clearly dangers of their usurping the rights of the wider society. (This is crucial. I touched upon it in the previous chapter and will return to it later). They will, from their professional expertise, have considerable knowledge of what is appropriate to teach at what stage—in the sense of what children are capable of learning. But this is quite different from granting them rights to determine the curriculum as a whole. Would it be appropriate for one section of society, albeit the teachers, to lay down the appropriate educational diet for society as a whole?

The case for the parents is a more plausible one. Sociologically it may be argued that the teacher's role is an extension of the parents' role. In a complex society the family can no longer serve as the unit through which the child is initiated into the skills and knowledge thought to be necessary and desirable for participation in adult society. Thus special institutions, schools, are provided and special individuals, teachers, paid to do just this. Yet these schools are not provided nor are the teachers paid just by the parents. This is of course a matter of fact and not a philosophical point. But as they are not thus appointed it may be thought that the right to lay down curricula lies not just with parents but with society as a whole.

Should then society as a whole decide? There are problems here. Talk of 'society deciding' easily suggests some sort of supra-personal metaphysical reality, 'society', living a life of its own untouched by the lives of the individuals who comprise it. But if we are careful not to be trapped by such notions as this, it is of the nature of democratic societies that *ultimate* judgment on fundamental matters lies with the eletorate. And one utterly fundamental matter is the content of the education provided at public expense.

I realize that I am on very dangerous ground here. It might be pointed out, for example, that in Britain traditionally a great deal of control has been left to the teachers. I have no wish to deny this as a matter of fact. But the important term is 'left to'. If the electorate as a whole choose to leave it to the teachers—even though tacitly accepting their control—then so be it. My suggestion is merely that conceptually it is in the very nature of a democracy that the decision lies with society as a whole. This need not be taken as dogma however. The whole point of this book is to give the reader the confidence to analyse arguments in education and show up their faults and my own arguments should be no exception to this.

My general arguments here should not be taken to imply that all questions of curriculum content are wide open. Many elements among what has traditionally been taught are unlikely in practice to be questioned for one moment. Who would suggest that children should not be taught to read for example? But there are nevertheless many areas where radical change has been advocated in recent years and where radical changes have in fact been taking place. In the early stages of mathematics for example, as I pointed out earlier, the emphasis on computation has been giving way to an emphasis on the inherent nature of mathematical processes. This might be thought to be a change which lay wholly in the field of the expert, the mathematician, to decide. Certainly much of the initiative for change lay here. But it is, I think, naïve to interpret the change simply as the substitution of good mathematics for bad mathematics and to suggest that what is going on is no business of anyone outside the sacred group of initiates. Behind it, as I argued, is an implication that certain skills, once necessary in society but no longer so, are not in themselves of any great inherent worth and that others have greater value. I believe, however, that the argument here should be public and that the experts should state their case and defend it rather than assume it. After all the very process of doing so is, in a wider sense, educative—both for the mathematicians and for the public. And, unless one believes that education is confined to what goes on in schools, that is itself an argument in its favour.

8. SUBJECT-CENTRED AND CHILD-CENTRED THEORIES

The discussion of worthwhileness in the previous chapter presumed that about any particular area of content, proposed for education at any stage, one might ask whether it was worth including. In considering this question it became clear that various general lines of defence could be put forward. Even if it is agreed that none of these establish an absolute, watertight case, it can still be considered whether some broad grouping can be considered preferable to some other. Frequently discussion here concentrates on two approaches which are contrasted, the child-centred and the subject-centred.

It will be clear that I am not talking here merely of a pair of hypothetical opposites—in fact I shall argue that there are theoretical difficulties involved in considering them as opposites at all. I am referring to parties and to partisans, to camps and to entrenched positions. Groups and individuals go forth into educational battle under the banner of child-centredness or subject-centredness. The terms have varying emotive tones according to one's presuppositions. The term 'child-centred' is frequently used interchangeably with the term 'progressive' which contains a positive evaluation as an inbuilt element—one could hardly be against progress. And the proponents of child-centred theories frequently accuse their opponents of being 'formal' which may perhaps be thought to have pejorative implications. On the other hand the defender of a subject-centred approach frequently accuses the child-centred theorist of being woolly minded and of failing to be concerned with standards. For him 'academic' is a hurrah word; for the child-centred theorist it may be a boo word.

Again the philosopher seeks not to declare a winner but to find out what the fight is about. It may prove that much of the opposition is more apparent than real. It is worth discovering what is really at stake and considering whether there are elements in the situation which can be resolved. Presumably unnecessary disputes are to be avoided if possible; tension can be fruitful but hardly so where there is nothing at stake.

Clearly the child-centred position is one which by its very nature is opposed to any view of worthwhileness which sees this as lying in the subject matter itself. The question, it is claimed, is not 'what is worthwhile?' but 'what is worthwhile *for this child*?' The value lies not in the thing, frequently described as inert (here a pejorative term), but in the unique inter-action of learner and material, of the child with the object *as experienced*. This is not a new idea; it can be traced through various educational theorists, finding an exceedingly powerful exposition in Rousseau's 'Émile' in the eighteenth century and, in England, deeply embedded in the Hadow Report of 1931. A frequent way of expressing the broad position is by saying that the needs and interests of the child are what should determine the content of the curriculum.

Some of the objection to this view may seem fairly obvious. One may for example ask what constitutes a need. Of course the child needs air and food and water and sleep—but what are his educational needs? The problem, glimpsed at earlier points in this book, is that of how we can enumerate any of these without taking a certain view of childhood and of what it is to be human, thus no longer being child-centred. For to build the whole of the educational provision on what the child saw as his needs is an enterprise which is difficult to envisage. Indeed, as an educational enterprise it seems to me actually to be self-contradictory, for the child can perceive his needs only within a social context—one keeps coming back to this point —and thus the nature of the context determines his view. Or, as it has been put in terms of 'interests', what interests the child may not be in the child's interests. He has to have needs created for him and interests developed.

The child-centred theorist tends to resist such a view because it looks to have within it elements of moulding, of adult authoritarianism and lack of respect for the values of childhood. But one has to ask whether it is not logically inescapable that adults have to make some decisions about what should constitute the content of the child's education. A child cannot just learn, he has to learn something; he cannot just experience, he has to experience something; he cannot even just develop, he has to develop in certain directions. And to fill in none of the content is, I suggest, not to educate but to abdicate. One could (logically) leave content to chance but I shudder to think of the consequences.

Looked at in a rather different way however it seems to me that there are at least three senses in which the child-centred view may be thought to be of value—I do not say that all these are senses in which the view is wholly right, but they are ones in which it deserves close consideration.

First it stresses that children matter as children. Childhood may be thought to be under-valued (to put it mildly) if it is seen simply as preparation for adulthood. If children (I include adolescents) are going to spend eleven or more years compulsorily in education there seems to be great distortion in regarding all this simply as a means to later ends. And personally here I would underline the child-centred theorist's values heavily.

Secondly the view stresses that the child can only learn what he can learn. By this I mean, quite simply, that whatever the

62

value of a particular experience it can be of no value to that child unless he experiences it, that if he is incapable at a particular point of learning in a particular area then it is, again quite simply, just a waste of time to try to teach him in it.

Thirdly the view stresses the importance of choice and open-endedness. When I say that adults must make some decisions on content I mean neither that they must make all decisions nor that they must be closed-ended in all that they do. A practical effect of much child-centred theory has been a thrilling expansion in the imaginative experience and the intellectual achievement of many children.

But its advocates do themselves an injustice when they describe their activities as though they were wholly determined by the children or when, as on occasion in practice, they let activity degenerate into the aimless and the trivial, in the false belief that only thus can they respect the integrity of the child.

Or has my argument been bogus? I have moved from analysis to advocacy. Does my analysis sufficiently support my advocacy?

I suggest that many of my points can be reversed in considering subject-centredness. As is so frequently pointed out the verb to teach has two objects. If one is taken away the expression is *always* incomplete. 'I teach Mary'; 'What do you teach her?'; 'Nothing, I just teach her'—quite meaningless! 'I teach algebra'; 'To whom do you teach it?'; 'To no one; I just teach it'—ditto.

Subject-centredness places all the stress on the material. It sees this as dominating the process. As value lies here, in the subject matter, the child has just to be brought to what is. His limitations in ability to perceive must simply be removed. The child's perception has value to the extent to which it reflects the adult's—this and this only. These are the stresses of subject-centredness. In practice the difference very often lies in the opening moves. 'Centredness' is reflected by whether one begins where the child is and leads him towards the subject or where the subject is and throws out a line. If my metaphors here have any validity then it may be fair to suggest that *seen in this way* it is the child-centred theorist who is right. It may now be protested that I had stressed that the philosopher did not referee. But thus the italics. By admitting this the subject-centred view has really nothing to lose.

It is really high time that all this talk of centredness disappeared for, given that it is correct that teaching *must* have two aspects, how can it be centred only on one of them? In this way it is a sham fight. The real dispute, I suggest, lies in the extent to which end-states are preconceived. The child-centred theorist is likely to regard the active involvement of children as of great value in itself and to be little worried by thought of where it may lead. He is ready to accept great variation in individual patterns of development, interests, values and degrees of organization. He will worry little about what is not known, believing that 'felt' gaps will be filled by the necessity of the stimulated on-going enquiry.

On the other hand, the subject-centred theorist puts a great deal of stress on the end-state. He tends to believe that there are certain things which all should know and that these exist in definite hierarchies, both logically and in degrees of worth-whileness. The child's mind must be enriched but it must also be sorted out. The sequence of historical events, mathematical processes, literary development must be followed. A child cannot just plunge in at any point, taking a stimulus as a starter and going wheresoever his interests take him, because he has no framework to help him to sort out the relevant from the irrelevant or to ensure understanding of earlier stages and necessary connections.

In part the difference between the two views may lie in deep underlying differences between their assumptions on the nature of knowledge. In part it seems to reflect their differing values: for one side the value lies in experience, engagement; for the other in achievement, accuracy. Again, it will be noticed, there is here a dispute about ends, not merely about the effectiveness of means. And such a dispute may be much harder to reconcile.

It is reasonable to suggest yet again however that one-sided interpretations look very distorted. The balance of importance beween involvement and end-state achievement may well vary from subject to subject—I suggest that it does. In any event there are a number of empirical questions regarding the effectiveness of techniques. Even if a clear, logical structure is taken as the ultimate end it does not *necessarily* follow that this is best taught or learned as a logical sequence; whether it should be is an open question. And the answer to this question may well vary not only with the nature of the subject but also with the age and/or ability of the child.

In this discussion I have referred repeatedly to subjects but it may well be asked what a subject is. Again, of course, to ask for the meaning of a word like this is not to suggest that one does not, in the ordinary sense of the word 'meaning', already know it. The question is more likely to be 'what *really* constitutes a subject?' The assumption is that one knows that various words are conventionally used, particularly on time-tables, to label portions of the work of a school, but is querying the nature of the analysis which leads to these words. Are they in fact distinct from one another? And do they leave important gaps?

It is fashionable—and this is one of the influences of child-centred theories—to attack subject divisions. It is frequently alleged that knowledge is essentially indivisible or that, to young children particularly, subject labels mean very little.

There is a peculiarly great danger in this area of confusing questions which should be kept distinct. For example, if one believes that there are clear and unarguable logical differences between subjects it does not follow that they should always and necessarily remain quite distinct on the time-table. Conversely, if one believes that there are difficulties in distinguishing subjects from one another and that there is a great deal of overlap, it does not follow that subject divisions have no place on the time-table at all.

Let us consider a fairly simple example. Historical factors are usually distinguished from geographical ones for many purposes. Very crudely indeed we might even wish to say that history was concerned with the dimension of time and geography with that of space. Yet clearly the two are connected. It can be argued that one could not possibly understand the military exploits of Napoleon without a clear understanding of certain geographical factors and, therefore, that separate teaching of geography and history is time-consuming and unreal. Numerous links of this kind can be shown. In any case, if an interest of the child is taken as a starting point, all kinds of development may occur. Suppose that the child begins with an interest (however aroused) in Napoleon. This may lead to work on the political structure of Europe (albeit embryonically), Europeon geography, military tactics (what 'subject' is this?), art appreciation, psychology (how can one speculate on motivational forces in Napoleon without considering them in general?), philosophy (was he justified in . . .?) and so on. This is unavoidable if the subject is really being followed up. And this would be so even for younger and less able children. We may not wish to refer to their psychological and philosophical enquiries but they will speculate on why he did what he did and whether he should have done!

From the subject viewpoint, however, it can be claimed, as I have indicated, that such enquiries are likely to be of little depth unless they are allowed to continue for their own sake.

To digress relevantly, the subject of education itself raises this kind of problem. If one wishes to deal with an educational issue then, as we have seen, it frequently appears to have a number of components. These cannot be sufficiently considered unless one has fair knowledge of psychology, sociology, philosophy and so on. Yet, it may be argued, if one deals with all these things separately there is a danger of losing the educational issue with which we were concerned.

I tend to think that there is no *one* approach which is always valid. At times topics may link subjects; at times subjects may be pursued in isolation. But we still have not clarified what a subject is.

One way of trying to do this is by considering logical differences between types of claims which are made. I referred to such differences briefly at an earlier point. For example mathematical propositions are logically different from scientific ones. Suppose that I refer to Pythagoras' Theorem in Euclidean geometry. The claim that the square on the hypotenuse of a right-angled triangle is equal to the sum of the squares on the other two sides is a claim of a particular kind; it is a claim that this is necessarily true, that it could not be otherwise. Mathematicians are not awaiting the possible appearance at some future date of a right-angled triangle of which this is not true. It is understood that the nature of the proposition is such as to guarantee its truth. Scientists, by contrast, can make no such assumpions. The fact that matter of a certain kind has been shown to behave in a certain way in certain circumstances leaves it *logically* open that in future some differences may be observed. Of course predictability is in fact assumed in normal circumstances, but the fact that matter behaves consistently, in this sense, does not alter the fact that statements about its behaviour are quite different from those about the characteristics of right-angled triangles.

Attempts to catalogue subjects in this way are fraught with difficulty however. Are religious statements wholly different in kind from all others? Are historical statements wholly distinct? In any case, many conventional school subjects do not correspond with such distinctions at all. School subjects seem to be largely devices of convenience; thus, like all such, the question can be asked, how convenient are they? And, again, there is no one answer. At times they may be thought indispensable, at others a fundamental hindrance to understanding.

The point about *logical* differences is not so much, perhaps, that they should be reflected in the structuring of a time-table but that they should be recognized in all teaching and that, however work is organized, learning should be true to the nature of the material learned. If children come to think that something is absolutely and undeniably true when in fact it is speculative, undemonstrable or unprovable, then both the child and the subject-matter are outraged. But such a claim, strong though it is, does not entail any one form of organization.

It may have been noted that there has been a tendency in the foregoing argument to regard education as concerned with knowledge. Many aspects of the curriculum however are not fundamentally concerned with knowledge at all or, at least, not with knowledge of propositions. This is true whether or not one regards oneself as child-centred, or subject-centred (bogus though this is as a rigid dichotomy). I have just distinguished between knowledge and one of its divisions, knowledge of propositions. I know that three multiplied by seven is twenty-one; I know that Charles II ascended the throne in 1660 though dated his reign from the execution of his father;

I know that the formula for water is H_2O; I know that deciduous trees are those which lose their leaves in autumn. All these are propositions, though the tests for truth in each case are different (you may wish to consider them). But it is a mistake to think of education as equivalent to learning that (and thus 'coming to know that').

In addition to learning 'that' children learn 'how'. Some people might wish not to call this knowledge at all but to take such a view is to run counter to usage; we speak normally, for example, of 'knowing how to swim' or 'knowing how to ride a bicycle'. These activities themselves we refer to as skills. 'Knowing that' and 'knowing how' are by no means always sharply distinguishable however. In order to know how to read a child has to know that certain responses are called forth by certain stimuli. In order to know how to make correct mathematical calculations, he has to know that certain mathematical formulations are correct. We refer to complex skills such as 'being able to think scientifically' which are quite inconceivable without a great deal of scientific knowledge.

This latter point is of particular significance. I referred earlier to my own view that education should stress method more and content less. But method cannot exist without content. One cannot know how to think scientifically without knowing any science or how to think historically without knowing any history. How far, however, one has to be conscious of exactly what one knows in certain areas of skill is doubtful. If one has learned how to ride a bicycle for example what does one 'know that'? That one has to transfer weight to counteract the lean of the machine? It might be said that whether one has learned this or not is not a matter of whether one can state that this has to be done—utter the true proposition—but simply of whether one can do it. In other words the knowledge is shown by the action. Is this sufficient? Or does one have to be able to state the principle in some way? And what are the implications of one's answers for teaching a skill? Can one simply learn by imitation—the 'watch me and then do the same' technique? This may be thought to depend on the nature of the skill. Where physical movements are fundamental there would seem at least to be something in it. But one could hardly learn the skill of reading in that way. Further consideration of different skills will show the great difficulty of valid generalization.

The verb 'know' also takes the direct object and I suspect that this aspect of it is too often neglected in education. If I am asked whether I know Brahms' Fourth Symphony I am being asked whether I have experienced it. I am certainly not just being asked whether I know that he wrote a fourth symphony. And I am not being asked anything about it. I could certainly reply for example, that I did not know it very well, meaning that I had not heard it often, that I was not familiar with it. Or I might reply that I know it well but that I do not know much about it. On the other hand it would be possible for someone to reply that he knows that it was composed in 1885, that it is in the key of E minor and that the fourth movement is a set of variations, but that he does not know the symphony at all. By this he means simply that he has never heard it.

When I say that I suspect that knowing plus direct object is too often neglected in education I mean that the emphasis on learning, knowing how and knowing that, can lead to a neglect of direct experience. Partly this may stem from a neglect of the teaching/teacher distinction already discussed. Teachers believe that it is, by definition, their job to teach. Teaching implies learning. Therefore unless their pupils learn they are not doing their job. Thus runs the argument. But I have suggested that it by no means follows from the fact that someone is called a teacher that the only activity they can legitimately engage in, in their professional capacity, is teaching as such. They may well, *at times*, seek to bring their pupils into direct contact with varying experiences leaving it as an incidental what, or indeed whether they learn. Clearly this can easily be exaggerated. But there may be times when children hurry round beautiful buildings with their questionnaires, learning about them, and fail to experience the entity at all.

Granted that we may bring children to know about things, teach them how to do things, bring them into direct contact with things, so that they know that, know how, and know, what else may be involved in the educational process? I referred in passing earlier to the distinction between knowledge and belief and to the question whether beliefs can be taught. Or rather the question is whether they should be, for certainly it is possible to do so. The question of the distinction between knowledge and belief is a particularly difficult one philosophically. If we were able to divide propositions sharply into those which we could know to be true and those which we could only believe to be true then it would be easier to argue a clear-cut educational case for differences in treatment. But we can make no such clear distinction.

Before seeing broadly why we cannot, I must ask why we should want to do so anyway. This book is not concerned with playing with words for the game's sake but with investigating problems which involve those concerned with education in practical difficulties. In this area the problem is that many people would say that we should only teach those things which we know, or, at least, that if we only believe something, we have no right to teach children that it is the case. Probably it is in the area of religious education that the problem arises most acutely. It is argued, for example, that a proposition such as 'that Christ is the Son of God' can only be believed to be

71

true and not known to be true and thus that it should not be taught as if it were true. Others however would say that for them this is the one supremely important proposition; they might claim also that they *know* it to be true and query why they could possibly be asked to refrain from passing on this, to them, supreme truth to others.

Broadly, distinctions between knowledge and belief can be considered as being concerned with tests for truth. If I claim to know that something is the case it is reasonable to ask me how I know. Suppose that the subject of the question is that five multiplied by seven is equal to thirty-five. I appeal to the nature of mathematics and to conventional number meanings. I know because I understand the process. It could not be otherwise. It is an example of what philosophers call an *a priori* proposition, that is one of which the truth is evident if one understands the meaning of its terms. One simply does not need outside evidence. Suppose that I am asked how I know that magnets attract iron filings. I might of course reply that I know because someone whom I trust has told me so. But the test is to produce a magnet and show that it attracts iron filings, it is an *empirical* test. (Actually, in this case, it might be argued that the power to attract iron filings could be regarded as a defining characteristic of a magnet so that the answer would be 'I know because that is what a magnet is'.) Consider then how one knows that sugar dissolves in water. Or I might be asked how I know that Cairo is in Egypt. The answer is 'from the atlas', but I could, in principle, go and check up. I could not however check directly on the 'fact', for example, that Shakespeare wrote 'Hamlet'. I have to take this on the basis of evidence. And the evidence can be, and of course has been, doubted. Nevertheless the proposition is normally taught as true.

We may gradually see knowledge tailing off into belief however in various areas. For example consider questions concerned with the motivation of characters in history. Children are frequently told that A did B because he wanted X, when no one could seriously claim that they *know* that he wanted X. It is a fair judgment in the light of the evidence that we have but it is belief rather than knowledge.

Why then is there such a severe problem over religious education? Fundamentally, I suggest, it is because of the degree of importance attached to the view taken and the degree of freedom allowed—or not allowed, in the questioning of the view. If a child questions the accuracy of a historical statement, even one concerning whether a particular event took place at all, he is not thereby questioning all historical accuracy (if he does this he is either unbalanced or a prospective philosopher!). Similarly if he requires the accuracy of a result in a scientific experiment he is not querying scientific procedures in general. If the validity of a mathematical proof is doubted, it is assumed that procedures of proof in general are being taken for granted; what is in question is applicability in a particular instance.

By extension, if a particular element in a religious position is queried, then this is more likely to be welcomed than otherwise as a sign of an enquiring mind, though this would have been far from so in earlier times, and in some places today doubtless all questioning in this area is regarded as unfortunate. The real problem is the possibility of doubting the validity of *all* religious statements. It is not even possible to conceive of what would be meant by denying the validity of *all* mathematical, scientific or historical statements—except in the case of a total philosophical scepticism. But many regard religious statements as having no objective validity, thus consigning them to the world of belief at least or even of nonsense. By 'nonsense' here I mean, literally, non-sense. For such people there could be no such subject as religious knowledge. There could however be such a thing as religious education, for one could educate children *about* the religious views which men have held or hold without making any presumptions at all concerning their validity.

To do this only, however, would, for many, be to omit the one thing that matters—what they regard as the truth, the supreme truth of a particular view. A number of compromise solutions have been put forward in this area; few command any degree of agreement. Official reports normally have recommendations which are actually self-contradictory (the reader may like to look at the relevant parts of the Plowden and Newsom reports). But enough has been said to highlight the broad nature of the problem and, again, to help the reader guard against the more facile of the pronouncements made on this subject.

Knowing that, knowing how, knowing (experiencing), believing—these aspects have been looked at. But they seem very passive. 'Learning how' may involve activity but activity here is judged as a means to an end. Has it no more positive a role than this? Is it not an end in itself? The term 'activity methods' is certainly very much a part of the 'in' educational vocabulary. The word 'methods' suggests that activity is seen as a means to an end. Clearly, however, many teachers now regard activity as, in some sense, important in itself.

We have to beware of too easy an identification of activity with physical activity. We cannot measure the activity in a school, in any educational sense, by measuring the degree of movement. Movement may be quite aimless and purposeless. It is a thoughtless person who condemns a child for passivity if he is sitting with a book or even if he is watching television. Not only may the child be mentally active but he may actually be participating in the sense that his own thinking is in inter-action with that of the writer or the producer of the programme.

One considerable element in education however may properly be thought to be physical activity of various kinds and another to be creative activity. A variety of physical skills may be developed, some, but by no means all, concerned with games. In many quarters there is developing a growing concern for movement as such, for its own aesthetic values, and for the emotional and imaginative stimulus that it can be. The same kinds of questions can be asked about this as about any other subject in the curriculum.

There are a particular set of questions however which are raised by the concept of creative activity or creativity (not that I am equating these two terms). There are a number of areas within which it is being urged that children should not only be active in learning, in coming to know and to appreciate, but in creating. Painting, of course, has been a very common element in the curriculum and the move from the dominance of the representational into freer expression is so familiar that it is now scarcely remarked upon. In other areas however there is growth of activity on a large scale; among these are three-dimensional art, 'creative writing' and music-making. This is not a book on current developments in education. My purpose is limited to asking what general questions arise here.

Basically they are concerned with the value of these activities. Can we say that if they give the children pleasure and enjoyment then this alone is sufficient justification for their inclusion in the curriculum? Some teachers talk as if this were so. But in what sense is this educational? Or can one argue that just as everything which occurs validly in a school need not be teaching and learning, so it need not be educational? (Not, of course, if its occurring in a school makes it educational by definition but this I think is ruled out—why?)

Others may find justification of these activities as stepping-stones to later development. Is their value in the product? Is the worthwhileness of practical music-making simply a function of the worthwhileness of the music made? Can participation itself be regarded as valuable?

Again a series of questions. But too often in the past the content of the curriculum has been as it is simply because questions have not been asked. And it may now be that innovations occur simply when individuals combine enthusiasm with powers of organization. The questions of justification have to be asked. That they are hard to answer makes them more important.

We are now ready to consider issues which are raised by those who regard the traditional subject divisions as restrictive yet recognize that the learning of children requires some kind of focus. Frequently it is suggested that learning should be centred on some kind of theme or topic or project upon which the various 'subjects' will be brought to bear. These 'centres of interest' can operate for an individual, a group, or a class as a whole; the actual working-out can take and may take many forms. The questions to be asked however remain those which we have been asking hitherto. Is there anything worthwhile in the topic itself? Are there incidental worthwhile achievements, by-products of the process? Is the child's interest in the topic sufficient justification? Is justice being done to the nature of the subject matter?

Let me take a specific example. A child is busily engaged on an individual project; he is writing a history and general survey of his favourite football club. Is this in itself to be regarded as worthwhile? Has one's view of the worthwhileness or otherwise of football any great relevance to the issue? Would it be more worthwhile if he were studying the history of the office of Prime Minister? Or of St. Paul's Cathedral? Or of space flight? What may be emerging incidentally? Is the quality of the written work important? Let us suppose that he has reproduced the club's coat of arms exceptionally well, that he has drawn impressionistic paintings of players in action, that he has related dates of significance in the history of the club to national and international events, that he has drawn a detailed map of the situation of the ground and a detailed plan of the ground itself, that he has involved himself in mathematical calculations regarding results, that he has analysed samples of soil from the pitch and that he has written accounts of what he imagines it is like to be a player on a big occasion. How worthwhile is all this? Can its value be judged in isolation? If not, what else would be required?

How far may co-operation with others be thought to matter? Is it an end in itself or only to be judged by its efficacy as a means to other ends?

Answers to these questions may well depend in part on our scale of values. But to say that differences of opinion will occur is not to say that enquiry of a serious and detached kind is unimportant. Certain of the issues are conceptual. For example many procedures which involve the linking of subjects are being graced with the name of 'inter-disciplinary enquiry'. Here perhaps it should be asked why enquiry is being regarded as superior to instruction and what is involved in an enquiry being inter-disciplinary. Some are concerned with whether any enquiry can, logically, be inter-disciplinary unless the nature of the contributory disciplines is understood. And we may note that words such as 'integrated', 'connected' and 'wide' tend to have positive emotive force (they are 'hurrah' words) whereas 'separated', 'disconnected' and 'narrow' have a negative force. We can ask why this is so and whether it necessarily follows that certain educational procedures are right. If the general outcome of our thinking is to make us more cautious in our particular judgments, this is to the good.

9. THE 'AIMS' OF EDUCATION

So far I have referred to a number of aims which participants in the educational process may enunciate and may claim as aims about which they are concerned. On occasion such aims may be referred to not as though they were particular aims within the educational process but as though they were the proper aims of education itself. Thus, for example, it may be claimed that the aim of education is to develop the potential of all individuals or to educate the whole man.

The word 'aim' is itself worth some consideration. If something is claimed as *the aim* of education then it would look as though it was being included in the definition of the term education. If not, then clearly it is a recommendation; it is a statement of what the person concerned would like educationists to be aiming at. And it would be better described as the target than as the aim. Personally I would prefer to say that education as such has neither aims nor targets; educators however may have targets at which they aim.

There is an odd ambiguity about the concept of an aim. If I were to ask someone what his aim was in playing chess there are two quite different, though equally valid types of reply that he might give. He might, for example, say that it was to checkmate his opponent; he might say that he was relaxing and forgetting the worries of his work. The first is his aim once he has started to play the game, assessed within the context of the game itself; the second is his aim in playing the game at all. Genuine confusion arises in this area. Negative play in various sports is frequently defended on the grounds that the aim of playing is to win and attacked on the grounds that the aim is to give enjoyment. Both are correct statements of aim but of a quite different kind.

It can be seen therefore that when someone states the aim of a particular educational activity, he may be referring to the target at which the activity is aimed, the end-state which will be achieved if the activity is successful. This is analogous to checkmate or to scoring more points than your opponent. But he may be referring to the general values of the activity taken as a whole. The reader may like to consider how this relates to the distinction between the instrumental and the intrinsic made earlier.

How does this apply to attempts to lay down aims for education as a whole? If, for example, the fullest possible development of every individual's potential is stated as the aim, it might, I suppose, be thought that an end-state is referred to. But how could one conceivably measure whether it had been achieved? (It is very doubtful, incidentally, whether it could be achieved at all because development in certain areas may preclude development in others.) It looks much more as though what is being suggested is that the principle of seeking to develop individual potential must be borne constantly in mind. In one sense it is difficult to see how it could be forgotten. What could be an education which did not develop the potential of individuals? Here, however, one can note the stress on the development of *everyone's* potential and one realizes that what is being put forward is in fact a recommendation for an egalitarian rather than a hierarchical approach. Now we have something which can be regarded as much more specific and disputable.

What of 'the education of the whole man'? Clearly this is a catchphrase. But it embodies the notion that varying aspects of man's nature must be catered for, rational and emotional, intellectual and imaginative, or, as it is sometimes expressed, physical, mental, moral and spiritual. All these are grandiose terms however which themselves require close analysis. Basically, to speak of educating the whole man is to be translated into particular recommendations before it can be properly assessed. It is a neat—too neat—summary of certain stock attitudes as it stands, and it tends to command assent by its own 'hurrah' tones—who would wish to advocate the education of part men?! When the particular recommendations are sought it is realized that they must involve complex questions of the balance of the curriculum at various stages which cannot be pushed on one side by slogans and catchphrases.

It may perhaps be argued that I am being unfair to castigate these global 'aims' so severely. Pleas for the education of the whole man, it may be said, are pleas for the postponement of specialization or for avoidance of undue specialization. But until what point should specialization be postponed and what constitutes *undue* specialization? Many utterances in this area are almost empty of meaning. A speaker can produce widespread assent by arguing that he is opposed to too much specialization or that he would prevent premature specialization. It may not immediately be recognized that no one could conceivably disagree with him. Everyone is necessarily opposed to *too* much of anything; the word 'too' here means 'more than there should be'. Similarly, 'premature' here means 'before the correct time', so one *must* be opposed to premature specialization. The real questions of course are 'how much is too much?' and 'what is the correct time?'

Many discussions of the proper concern of education are concerned with the distinctions, or alleged distinctions, between reason and emotion. Various analogous though not identical pairings may appear: the cognitive and the affective; the mind and the heart; thought and feeling. Again one has to beware of clear-cut distinctions. Sometimes it is maintained that education should be concerned only with the cognitive—with understanding, knowledge, the training of the mind, the development of thought processes, the powers of reason. It is difficult to conceive, however, what could be meant by an education which paid no attention at all to the emotions, to the affective aspects of learning, for these are intricately inter-woven with the cognitive. Education must foster care and concern; how conceivably could it be otherwise? And do we not want people to feel excited by learning, to become emotionally aware, to gain happiness from new experiences, even to love the rational?

For many the problem seems to be that concern with the emotional seems to by-pass reason and to open up thoughts of indoctrination, of 'playing with man's feelings'. This, however, is only because too sharp a distinction is made at the beginning between the two areas. People's emotions and their understanding do not operate in watertight compartments having no relationship with one another. Even a deep concern for rationality can be regarded as emotional (it is certainly a strongly emotional concern for me). The vital questions are those concerned with the means by which the emotions are educated. And if we regard them as being *educated*, immediately the cognitive side is brought in, for, if they are educated rather than conditioned, this involves thought about their objects. Emotions are not free-floating; they are related to situations and to the ways in which these situations are perceived. I may feel nauseated by some situation; this is a factor of the nature of the situation *as I perceive it*. The cognitive and the affective are inseparable in practice.

Pleas for the education of the whole man may also contain elements concerned with a balanced subject curriculum. Although questions regarding the point at which specialization should be regarded as premature are complex, there are certainly wide differences of view. But again these come back to differences in the views of worthwhileness. Some would argue that any educated person (hurrah term) must (in order to be such) have some understanding of each of the main areas of human achievement. But how much? And has he to have interest as well? And, if so, how deep must this interest be? And what are our measuring rods for the depth of interest? In any case, is it in accordance with usage to *define* 'educated' in this way? Or is it a stipulative definition? Does it matter that a man should have breadth of understanding?

Some would wish to make it matter instrumentally rather than intrinsically. They would argue, for example, that breadth is required if men are to communicate with one another adequately. The politician is, by definition, distinct from the scientist, but he has to have some understanding of science in order to make appropriate decisions. If this is the case however, it may be arguable that it shows only that some scientific training is required as an integral part of his preparation for being a politician.

Others argue that breadth is required as a basis for choice. If specialization occurs too early, they argue, (again note *too*), then there are inadequate grounds for the choice of the area of specialization. This is a very powerful argument. But it is always one of degree. One could argue that the only way to know what is really involved in any area is to become fully involved in it and this is simply not possible. We cannot be committed to everything.

Again, it will be realized, my suggestion is that the particular practical decisions can never be absolutely justified, but will vary from case to case. If a strong specialist interest appears to manifest itself in a child at an early age this may be one ground for early specialization, particularly if, as a matter of fact, early specialization appears to be required for mature excellence (as is alleged in the case of violin playing for example).

Clearly the longer one postpones specialization the longer are options kept open. And we tend to commend a person who has wide interests. We regard his life as being richer. Certainly, too, there are prima facie grounds for supposing that a person who has received a broad education is likely to be more open to change, to be more flexible. And there are factors in modern society which clearly make flexibility desirable. So the general trend is against early specialization. I have been concerned only with showing that, as with so many other educational issues, the arguments may not all run one way.

The argument for breadth is sometimes expressed in terms of the alleged need for a liberal education. It will be noticed that liberal, like broad, has a positive emotional tone. It is associated with freedom, with lack of restriction. But those who use the term are by no means necessarily agreed upon what they mean by it. At times the basic idea seems to be the liberating force of understanding; the assumption is that the more one understands the freer one is to act. Ignorance and misunderstanding are confining forces. Thus a liberal education is one which gives a person scope through increasing the range of his grasp. At times the term seems to carry with it implications of 'learning for its own sake', of the importance of intrinsic worth. In this sense the term liberal is opposed to the term utilitarian; things are to be judged by their worth rather than by their usefulness. The earlier discussion of worthwhileness should help to throw some light on the helpfulness of this distinction.

Frequently 'liberal' is contrasted with 'vocational' and those who wish to increase the element of contrast tend to do so by referring to liberal education and vocational training.

This contrast of education and training is intended to reinforce the alleged difference between the liberal and the vocational. The suggestion is that processes of education carry with them an understanding of their nature and a considerable degree of concern for their ends. Training, on the other hand, suggests fixed ends and narrow concerns, a total stress on technical efficiency. If a person is being trained to do something, then one may infer that the nature of the something is not in question. Circus animals are trained to perform tricks; they are not educated.

If one then qualifies training with the adjective 'vocational' one has a clear implication of a narrowly conceived 'job' for which the person is receiving a preparation concerned only with technical efficiency. Linguistically this is very interesting for the noun 'vocation' has no such implication of narrowness. We commend a sense of vocation, regard it as being associated with a deep concern for ends, and tend to use it particularly in association with the priesthood, medicine and the higher academics.

We may now ask what proper distinctions there are to be made in this area. I suggest that different dimensions are being confused because of a failure to distinguish content from method. Narrow methods of teaching, devoid of concern for understanding, might be used on a wide-ranging curriculum. Thus, though broad, the education being received is in one sense clearly illiberal. On the other hand a professional or vocational course may be imbued with a deep concern for understanding and a readiness to ask fundamental questions about ends, in which case it is clearly liberal. I have no more right than anyone else to stipulate definitions. One can only listen carefully to the entire context of a person's expression of view and seek to refine what is being said. Too often a view sounds plausible merely because adjectives like 'liberal',

84

'broad', 'integrated' are being used to describe it; they pre-judge in its favour. One has to separate the issue of breadth of content from that of liberality of method and one has to ask what is the proper concern of the course in question. Frequently it is assumed that breadth and liberality are all-important and that technical efficiency is of virtually no account. But, at this moment, as I write, my car is undergoing repair at the garage and, however concerned I may be for general value, I hope that the mechanic working on it is technically efficient! And, if I am to have an operation, I require a technically efficient surgeon. For his sake, as a man, I hope also that he has had a liberal education, which enables him both to consider the wider implications of his vocation and to have a range of other interests and concerns. But unless he is technically efficient I shall be in trouble and so, in a different sense, will he!

The point is of interest with regard to the change of name of the British institutions for the professional preparation of teachers from Training Colleges to Colleges of Education. The change is in my view justified, for a teacher should be concerned with ends, should be self-critical, should be flexible in his view of the situation with which he is dealing, should have a depth of understanding of the processes involved. But this is not to say that there are no elements of training, of concern with sheer technical efficiency in prescribed areas. This is surely a proper element in the education of a teacher. Breadth and liberality are linked in the minds of many people with activity, participation and involvement. Severe strictures are laid upon courses which are alleged to be too passive as far as the learner is concerned. Desk-bound, book-bound, teacher-dominated—these are terms of abuse. It is frequently alleged that unless one is actively involved in the educational process as a learner then it is worse than useless. I have already suggested that there are grave dangers in equating activity with physical movement. Here I wish to add that one's understanding of a situation and one's perception of it are closely linked. It is frequently argued by student teachers that their *real* learning occurs when they are on practice in schools—and the implication is that all else is unreal. Yet what is often forgotten is that what is perceived in a school by an observer or a participant is a function of what he is prepared to perceive. The trained observer frequently feels that things which he notices simply could not be missed; he finds them shatteringly obvious. Yet frequently they would not have been noticed at all if it had not been for his previous preparation.

We can extend from this into further consideration of the whole nature of the relationship between theory and practice. It is an important feature of this to consider the emotional associations of these terms themselves. If we say that someone is practical then normally, I think, we are praising him. We simply do not say of someone that he is theoretical. We may say something like 'it's all theory with him', and if we do this, we are being adversely critical; the suggestion is that his thought never gets him anywhere. The adjective 'mere' is often associated with theory to denigrate more strongly; we do not normally speak of 'mere practice'. Thus there seems to be an inbuilt assumption that practice is superior to theory, inbuilt that is within the nature of the language itself. Yet I believe this to be misleading. We often speak also of the practical man as someone who knows what he is doing and I suggest that when we do this we are also assuming that he has good reason for doing it. This, however, is to say no more than that there is a theoretical basis to his activity. What could be a greater waste of time than to spend a vast amount of effort and energy upon something and then to decide that it was not worth doing anyway?

Some of the opposition to theory doubtless springs from fear.

It is often uncomfortable to question the methods one is adopting in one's practice; it may be no less than traumatic to go a stage further and query whether the practice is worthwhile at all.

There is much misunderstanding in this area. A frequently used phrase is 'it is all right in theory but it does not work in practice'. The point of such theory however is that it should guide practice. If it does not work in practice then it is *not* all right in theory. Of course theories are, by their very nature, general. Their application in practice involves a great deal of thought about the particular circumstances of the particular case. And frequently a claim that a theory does not work in practice is no more than the reaction of impatience to a difficult set of circumstances or of a failure to adapt the theory in the light of the situation. One must repeat however that a theory that could not work in practice is simply a bad theory.

I am speaking here, of course, of those theories which are intended to guide practice. There are theories which are explanatory of phenomena, theories for example which are concerned with the origin of the universe, which do not have this function at all. My remarks are simply not concerned with these.

Theories, in the sense with which I am concerned, are the grounds for practice. They are statements regarding the justification of intended aims of the practice and the means to be adopted to further these. Thus all practice *must* have some theoretical background, even if this is assumed. In an activity as complex as education we cannot afford to make assumptions. The problem for the theorist is that the more general his theory, the less relevant it may seem to be in practice. But the crucial word is 'seem'. For a demand for relevance can easily become a demand for narrowness. If the ends of a process are assumed, then relevant theory can be concerned only with the means of achieving them. And this *seems* practical. Whereas if the ends are questioned relevant theory must range much more widely. And questioning ends brings us back to general statements of aim. Inevitably one has returned again to this point. It is a strange paradox of much radical protest that in demanding relevance in courses it is in danger of a conservatism which is the very opposite of what is really wanted by the protesters themselves.

We are now ready for a further look at the components of educational theory. In considering them I am not, of course, concerned with the reporting of empirical evidence. I am concerned with the kind of contribution which can be made by different aspects of theory, with their own theoretical assumptions and with the nature of their relationship with one another.

10. THE DISCIPLINES OF EDUCATION

Immediately one asks what are the components of an educational theory one is in difficulties. For the terms which are used to describe these suffer from all the limitations of other such terms in their vagueness of usage on the fringes and their openness to a variety of stipulative definition. One is faced with difficulties of gap and of overlap. The main contenders for a place however are psychology, sociology, philosophy, history and comparative education. One can characterize these claims very crudely as follows: education is concerned with people and therefore information about the behaviour of people is theoretically relevant to it (psychology); it occurs in a social and institutional context and thus an understanding of the operation of groups and institutions is required (sociology); it raises questions of aims, intentions and justification and of clarification of concepts (philosophy); it has dimensions in time (history) and space (comparative studies). I repeat that this is, deliberately, very crude. There are no refined definitions here. But it is sufficient to delineate very rough areas and to establish prima facie claims.

I stated earlier that when philosophy 'spawned' its offspring, mathematics, the sciences, the social sciences, it did not thereby solve all the philosophical problems in those areas. Each of them has its own philosophy. And philosophical psychology is an exceedingly important area of study concerned with the status and justification of psychological claims. When I refer to their status I am not of course using the term in any sense concerned with relative importance. I refer simply to their logical nature. Can they be proved true? What assumptions are made? What procedures are necessary in order to verify them?

Some psychologists wish to claim for their study the full status of a science (and perhaps I should admit that there is some element here of status in the other sense). By this they mean broadly that the views put forward have no element of personal opinion about them and are publicly verifiable by agreed procedures of observation, experiment and measurement. Just as a scientist observes the behaviour of chemicals or of basic particles of matter or of plants, so the psychologist observes the behaviour of human beings—no more and no less. As with many other issues which I have considered in the space of a few paragraphs, but concerning which volumes have been written, I can do no more here than raise a few crucial questions. In observing the behaviour of a human being the psychologist is observing complex phenomena. Behaviour, for him, will include everything that is observable. Thus physical reactions which are outside conscious control will be part of behaviour. Some of these may be of no interest to the psychologists but others, for example an increase of heart beat as a response to certain stimuli, may well be.

Those psychologists who choose to regard their study as the science of behaviour turn their backs upon the phenomenon of consciousness and upon all talk of mind and the mental. It is of course true that talk of mind poses immediate problems because, for all the normality of the use of the term, we have no object with which we can associate it. Yet the ordinary person thinks that his behaviour is certainly only part of the story and would stress that there are unconscious and conscious processes which are crucial to an understanding of behaviour. He might argue that if he carried through a particular action he might have done so almost unconsciously without prior thought, or intentionally after deep consideration and with serious misgivings. There may be clues in behaviour as to this but there may not be. The 'behaviourist' would not necessarily wish to deny this but would argue that all that is available to him to study is behaviour itself and that to infer from this why it is going on in any individual is to make a speculative and unscientific move.

Discussions of psychologists' methodology have been wide-ranging but we can only note here that differences in educational procedures may well result from differing views in this area. (Analogously differences in the treatment of the mentally ill frequently derive from fundamental differences regarding the nature of mind and of behaviour.) Learning, for example, may well be regarded as being demonstrable through changes in behaviour or even as definable in these terms. Those who take this view are likely to favour educational procedures which are clearly measurable in terms of their results. They may also tend to support procedures which see learning as a series of responses to different stimuli. And they will, to put it mildly, be suspicious of theories which speak of insight and understanding as phenomena to be studied. They will tend to be mechanistic and to be comparatively unconcerned about dangers of conditioning, perhaps even regarding education as simply a form of conditioning. Man is reduced to the same kind of phenomenon as all else studied by the scientist.

Opposing views tend to stress man's uniqueness. They emphasize the point that each individual human being has 'privileged access' to his own mental states, whatever the difficulties of the word 'mental'. They will urge that what is distinctive of being human is that we know what it feels like to be angry or excited, interested, bored, puzzled, confused, thwarted, anxious and so on and that our behaviour is secondary. They will stress that in learning there are questions not only of changes in behaviour but of insight and depth of understanding which can be described and analysed. They may well refer frequently to man's dignity and resent procedures which they regard as manipulative, as designed to change behaviour without full regard to the conscious consent and understanding of the person concerned. Personality may even be described as 'sacred' and certainly will be thought of as more than its constituent elements; a person is not merely (note the word) a collection of inherited and learned responses.

The nature of these disagreements is highly complex. Some may be no more than matters of procedural possibility, others seem to be right at the heart of man's view of himself, touching upon the metaphysical. Certainly some seem to involve value differences. For those who are concerned with what psychology can contribute to educational theory they pose fundamental difficulties. It might be thought that such differences were irrelevant here, that they lie only in the advanced views of the subject and do not impinge upon requests for practical help; but this is not so. Elementary texts tend to begin with a set of arguments for a view of psychology—or with a set of unstated assumptions. Quite a brief glance at such a book is likely to show whether or not its approach is behaviouristic. If one finds recurring references to stimulus and response, to conformity with norms, to the lack of significance of individual experiences in isolation, then one can infer the general nature of the line. On the other hand if one finds a stress upon understanding the individual, trying to break through to his consciousness, understand what he is feeling, gain imaginative insight into his condition, one can tell that one has a radically different approach.

It may help to illustrate from a specific and fundamental educational example, one which I have used earlier in a different context, the teaching of reading. Reading can be analysed in terms of behaviour alone. What is necessary is that the child should learn how to respond to a number of stimuli. These may be analysed into basic particles, letter shapes, but the required responses are complicated because they depend upon the context—how we respond to 'a' for example depends upon context (consider *plate*, *ran*, *cart*). Clearly however the whole procedure can be seen in mechanical and external terms; children are taught to respond correctly. There is no speculation about what is going on in their minds. Many teachers however might wish to say that it is precisely what is going on in their minds that interests them. If they suddenly spurt in achievement the teacher wants to know why and believes that to answer this he must have insight into the mental processes themselves, not merely into the consequent behaviour. To the behaviourist this is a myth from which we must release ourselves; to others—and I include myself— attempts to reduce all that is important in learning to be-haviour simply fail. Consciousness remains a phenomenon which is, above all others, known to us. To leave this out of account is to leave out the vital element.

It may well be argued that I have presented a caricature rather than a portrait. This is so. All brief presentations of this type are caricatures. But a caricature emphasizes key features and is recognizable. My main ground for attacking the be-haviourist approach is that it speaks of all behaviour in casual terms, necessarily so by its own terms. Many actions are perfectly well explained by their causes. But the philosopher is professionally interested in actions which are performed because of the reasons which people have for performing them and with the arguments which might be used to justify such actions. How may one observe from a man's behaviour that he is acting as he is because he has good reason to do so rather than because he is inescapably caused to do so? Reasons are explicated in language. And it is the capacity to speak which marks out the human being; he can give an account of his own actions. And he can speculate on 'why?' in two senses, for this word is highly ambiguous. It may be a request for a reason or it may be a request for a cause.

If a teacher punishes a child he may do so *because* he is in a bad mood or *because* the child deserves punishment. The first is a cause which could never justify, though it might explain the action; the second is a reason which can be objectively discussed. If it is thought to be justified (i.e. if the child did deserve the punishment) then this is so regardless of the particular person concerned. And men can consider these objective factors and make them operative in their behaviour. This can be described by saying that a man's reasons have become causally operative but this does not alter the fact that a reason is a very special type of cause.

Despite the broad questions which are raised by the approaches of psychologists it is, of course, abundantly clear that psychological enquiry has much to contribute to educational theory. In its scientific approach, psychology is concerned with generalization about human behaviour. Individual differences do not invalidate its conclusions; they merely prevent us from arguing infallibly from the generalization back to an individual instance. The stress upon language, which is one of the significant features of philosophical enquiry, is particularly important in consideration of the term 'normal'. Here is an instance where an unconscious move from a statement of the evidence to an inference which is unjustified is very frequent. If, as a result of an empirical investigation, certain behaviour patterns are shown to be normal at a certain age then clearly behaviour which runs counter to these is abnormal. But it is abnormal in a particular way; that is it is outside the range which *statistically* is normal. The problem is that the term abnormal suggests to us that something is wrong. In this case however it does not carry this meaning. It *may* be 'wrong' to be abnormal in this sense but it may not be; the question is open. But the ease with which the automatic yet mistaken inference may be made is obvious. This is an outstanding example of the care which is needed to interpret claims which, within their own terms, are perfectly proper; needless worry and anxiety may be avoided by a careful consideration of language. For a child's behaviour to be abnormal is perfectly normal; most of us are abnormal in some respect—there is no automatic assumption that this is 'cause for concern'.

In so far as psychologists provide explanatory models for human behaviour there are necessarily philosophical questions lurking and those concerned, in education, with use and interpretation of psychological evidence should be aware of them. One particularly potent problem is raised at any time when a claim is made in the form 'children of such and such an age can normally perform such and such an activity'. Any such claim raises very clearly the issue of the typicality of the children studied to children in general. For example if it were validated upon children in a well-to-do area of an urban community it would be possible that it would be true only of such. It would be absurd to describe all children in an isolated rural community in an underdeveloped country as abnormal if they were unable to do this. In other words claims are to be judged only within terms of the population sampled. The issue raises, however, not only the point of statistical validity but also, much more broadly, that of the effect of the environment upon achievement.

Any object of study is affected by environment. If a chemical element is the object of study then the atmosphere in which it is being studied (the degree of moisture for example) may be relevant; it may affect behaviour. There are problems however about considering human beings as organisms interacting with their environment in this sense alone. For the crucial element in human behaviour may be thought to be the inter-action of individuals with one another. We saw earlier that this factor made the analogy of the growth of a child with the growth of a plant a very limited one. A cabbage cannot persuade the next cabbage in the row to react to its environment differently! The work of the psychologist has thus to be supplemented by the work of the sociologist in studying inter-active systems. And as there is a vast area of overlap, the social psychologist is concerned particularly with the effects upon behaviour of the groups to which we belong.

This point may be put in another way. Any study of human behaviour *must* generalize; that is to say that from a study of John Brown in isolation nothing follows except in terms of John Brown. Not only is this so but it is not, as is so often suggested, a grave drawback that it is so. Indeed it can well be argued that it is in fact impossible to study John Brown in isolation anyway because the various things which we say about him are reflections of what we know about others. If we say that he is clever but lazy, good-humoured but prejudiced in some respects, these terms reflect our idea of the behaviour of others. So we imply norms by our language regarding the individual. The study of sociology reveals that the behaviour of any individual may be related not only to human beings as a whole, or to those of the same sex or the same age, but to those of similar social groupings. For example, the fact that a child comes from an urban working-class background may make him likely to show certain kinds of speech pattern.

Again it must be stressed that in this book I am not concerned with reporting any particular factual evidence at all but rather with assessing the status of the type of claim that is made. In an instance such as this we can see that such a claim would depend in part upon the definition that is taken for 'urban working class'. And we can see that whatever are here taken as appropriate criteria for membership of the urban working class, the conclusions drawn are valid if at all, only within the bounds of this definition. The justification for making the claim would simply be that it was true; that statistically it could be shown to be so. The dangers lie in interpretation.

Interpretation is likely to involve a move from a statement of correlation to a statement of cause. From the fact that two factors are found to 'go together' an inference is made that one is the cause of the other; the speech patterns of the children are as they are *because* they are working class children. This, of course, strictly goes beyond the facts themselves. Yet it seems to be what we wish to know; we are anxious to discover not merely *that* two factors are related but *how* they are related. Causal statements always require caution. They can be developed by further examination of distinct features of the situation and refined in this way. The most serious error, again, is to work back automatically from generalization to individual case: X is a member of the working class, therefore he will have the speech pattern in question. This is invalid. Even more serious is the error of assuming inevitability—the 'nothing can be done about it' attitude: 'the facts have shown us that . . . and therefore . . .' The vital question with human behaviour and with social groupings is that of how much can be altered. In education above all we are concerned with what is the case in order to change the situation in many ways. Description, explanation, prediction all have their parts to play but educational theory is not just the sum of these but a guide to practice.

The sociologist has a major contribution to make to the theory of education in terms of his study of social systems and groups. Men operate against a set of expectations which are not simply functions of the human organism or of the individual's genetic potential but of the particular environment created by nationality, social class, family expectations, religious affiliation and so on. A group is other than the sum of the characteristics of its members. The sociologist can help not only by studying group influences upon the children outside the educational system but upon those inside it also. Teachers and parents can be given aid in understanding how the structure of a class or a school operates and the effects which authority patterns, for example, have upon the development of individuals.

From the philosophical viewpoint, it is important to stress that a claim that 'a group is other than the sum of the characteristics of its members' is not some form of metaphysical claim that somehow the group has a reality apart from what its members do. Rather it is a shorthand form of saying that individuals' behaviour is greatly affected by the groups to which they have belonged and do belong and in which they are acting. Moreover there is a danger of assuming (this is frequently done I suggest) that the individual is only *really* himself when he is alone and that his actions with others are artificial. 'Real' is frequently a danger word to watch for in an argument. 'John often behaves like that but when you know him well you realize that he is not *really* like that.' His behaviour in question is as much part of reality as anything else, though a warning against assuming that it tells the whole story may well be in order. Returning for a moment to behaviourist assumptions in psychology, it is a reasonable point to make that there is great difficulty in sustaining any claim that a person is really different from his behaviour for this behaviour is at least part of his reality.

The stress upon social class in much sociological writing is a particularly likely source of confusion because of the emotive force of social class terms. The criteria which the sociologist chooses to mark off his categories may be objective, career structure for example may be taken as the crucial criterion, but it is very difficult for the layman to hold this stipulative definition in mind and not to interpret generalizations about the working class in a far wider sense or regard objective statements as evaluative condemnations.

A more general problem of both psychological and sociological studies, touched upon already, is the danger of their being interpreted in mechanistic terms; that is to say of assuming that statements regarding the way in which people do behave in certain circumstances or from certain social backgrounds somehow limit the freedom of individuals to do as they please. Such an interpretation is based upon a misunderstanding of the nature of the social sciences. Their generalizations are simply taken from what is observed. Even if given the name of 'laws', they are not telling anyone what to do. In this respect they are no different from scientific laws: the laws of planetary motion do not tell the planets how to behave; they describe how they do behave. This ambiguity in the concept of law is of fundamental importance. The laws of a country and the laws of science are quite different; the former are *prescriptions*—they say that certain things ought or ought not to be done, the latter are *descriptions*—they say that things occur in certain ways. And these descriptions form the basis of *predictions* on the assumption that, unless circumstances change, they will continue to act in these ways. Thus, when a sociologist argues that certain kinds of behaviour are likely to be observed in children from a particular environmental background, he is not saying that they must behave in this way or that they always will. He is making a judgment of probability in the light of the evidence.

Sociological enquiry has helped greatly in producing an understanding of group procedures and influences. But its status as scientific imposes limitations as much as it opens opportunities. It means that we can rely upon thorough work in the areas concerned but only within its own terms. The sociologist (like the psychologist) cannot tell us what ought to be because this is not the function of a scientist who is concerned with what is the case. In so far as sociologists or psychologists do pronounce on what ought to be they are going beyond their immediate role; they are acting not as specialists but as informed human beings and their judgments about the facts are open to challenge.

In using the word role in the previous sentence I used one of the sociologists' key technical terms. One of the areas of education which sociologists study is the role of the teacher. From this I can further illustrate my earlier point. The sociologist who studies the role of the teacher is not concerned with what teachers ought to do, which is an evaluation, nor with what is, or might be, *necessarily* or *conceptually* involved in teaching—a philosophical concern which we have already examined—but with what teachers actually do as teachers and with the ways in which in fact they characterize their activities. It is frequently suggested, for example, that Grammar school teachers see their role as different in many respects from the way in which Infant school teachers see their role. This is not a matter of objective differences in their tasks; there are obviously distinctions to be made here in terms of the nature of the work undertaken but it is not these which are at issue. Rather is it that the former tend to see their task as a limited intellectual one, the latter as a wider, personal one with heavy affective implications. And this is not an inevitable concomitant of age difference or general ability level of the children concerned. It would be quite possible for infant teachers to concentrate exclusively on basic skills and Sixth Form masters to concern themselves with the social welfare of their pupils.

The sociologist is concerned with patterns of behaviour which relate to group behaviour and with the effects of social structures upon behaviour and attitudes. What differences in values, for example, may be found between ex-pupils of an urban Comprehensive school and a rural Grammar school? How far do moral views of pupils correlate with authoritarian or democratic structures in their schools? How much agreement is there between what teachers aim for, what parents aim for, what teachers think parents aim for and what parents think teachers aim for?

The psychologist and the sociologist are both concerned with facts; the philosopher is concerned with concepts and their elucidation. Neither, as such, have any more right to make judgments of value than anyone else. But they too are full human beings as well as experts in an area. Generally they are careful to indicate when they are speaking outside the area of their professional competence. But this is not necessarily the case. And, even if the expert is himself careful, others may not be so careful in interpreting him. We must be careful about the judgments of experts within their own area of competence; beyond it we should be acutely careful. Among educational sociologists for example there are differences of opinion on the desirability of area comprehensive schools though 'the facts', such as they are, are open to all.

The area of the sociologist is particularly dangerous because it overlaps to such a degree with the areas of political controversy in education. Sociologists may study how comprehensive schools work, they cannot *qua* sociologists either advocate them or attack them. (The word 'qua' is very useful: to say that the sociologist cannot do such and such qua sociologist is to say that he cannot 'in his role as a sociologist'. In other words he takes off his professional garb to do so and has no expert authority to back his view.)

A very high degree of caution is required in assessing the validity of recent work in the sociology of knowledge. It is entirely proper for sociologists to ask why (causally) certain areas of knowledge are regarded as of educational significance in particular institutions at particular times and what the effects of these are. But some sociologists tend to pronounce upon what knowledge is or even to say what it ought to be taken to be in different areas. And their work here is extremely suspect.

A highly significant area of enquiry which sociologists have developed is that of the effects of the peer group upon behaviour. The child's peer group consists of his fellows of roughly the same age with whom he is in contact. Teachers frequently assume, as they teach, that the significant lines of relationship are a series of lines between the teacher and each individual. They recognize the existence of relationships within the class but may tend to regard them as irrelevant to or disruptive of their teaching. The sociologist can help to investigate these and their effect. A hypothetical example: a lively teacher may be working hard to arouse interest in an area and be depressed by his failure to do so. Why is he not 'getting through' to individuals? His assumption tends to be that something is wrong on the individual lines. But the trouble may be elsewhere. It may be thought to be 'against the group' to be interested, for example, in classical music. Thus each member may be trying not to be interested. Unless the teacher can counter the group view—or assumed group view —as such, he is unlikely to have success. Is this then a case where the sociologist's view can lead directly to a prescription? 'If you have difficulties in this area then you ought to investigate the group view and try to alter and circumvent it'—would there be anything wrong with such an argument? The danger lies in an assumption that the end is worthwhile and that means which reach it are justified. The teacher has always to ask first whether he is justified in doing what he is trying to do and whether, in attempting to reach his aims, he is offending against any moral principle or causing any side-effects which he would judge to be wrong. To put it very simply the expert cannot say 'you ought' but only 'probably you ought if . . .'

Historical and comparative factors can only here be touched upon. The current trend is towards giving both a strongly sociological interpretation. Thus historical studies investigate the inter-relationship between educational developments and other changes and factors in society at the time. In so doing there has, fortunately, been a decline in the tendency to say 'history teaches us that . . .' Circumstances alter cases. Particular events are rooted in their time. Education Acts like those of 1870 and 1944 in England must be judged in context. There are lessons to be learned from history; we can only learn from past experience. But they are not automatic. The study of what has been can never, of itself, tell us what should be. And this is for two reasons: first, that the circumstances are now different and second that we are making a judgment on the facts. Moreover the facts as presented are inevitably a highly selected sample. As with historical studies so with comparative studies. History does not 'teach us that'; neither does American experience or the evidence from Sweden—or the samples of these which are on offer. Both are rooted in other social contexts and both involve judgments of value. Insularity is absurd. We must study the experience of others. But social change and educational experience are hard to transplant; soils vary.

In sum, educational theory is an odd creature. It serves to constitute grounds for practice and as such it is based on facts. But the practice cannot strictly be deduced from the theoretical

H

facts educed in its support. There are always gaps. There are gaps of changing circumstance, gaps of doubt over the validity of evidence, and above all the gap between what is known to be and what, it is held, ought to be. The expert may describe with varying degrees of credibility and predict with varying degrees of probability. But he may not prescribe qua expert. The lesson of this is not that anyone's view is as good as anyone else's. The expert's view on what ought to be should be listened to seriously for he is likely to be seriously concerned in the area. But the legal principle of *caveat emptor* is a good analogy for the non-expert. Beware that what you are offered is within the capacity of the expert to supply.

11. EDUCATIONAL INSTITUTIONS
Discipline, Freedom, Authority and Responsibility

Consideration of sociological as well as psychological factors in educational theory is a reminder that educational processes occur in social contexts. In considering learning and teaching one might on occasion postulate a one-one relationship of teacher and learner. Yet even here it is a relationship which will involve factors other than the teaching intentions and skills of the teachers and the learning task. The teaching-learning relationship normally presupposes a personal relationship, however minimal.

In general, however, when considering education, we are presupposing the existence of an institutional framework within which the learning process is set. And many of the important theoretical questions are concerned with this setting as well as with learning within it. Frequently, for example, we speak metaphorically of the atmosphere of a particular teacher's classroom or of a school. So usual is the phrase that it is scarcely apparent that it is a metaphor. Philosophically the interesting question is, as so often, one of justification. What reasons might be put forward in favour of one atmosphere rather than another? For example let us consider a Primary school having two adjacent rooms with classes parallel in age and ability. One is marked by order, scrupulous tidiness, comparative sparseness of materials, quiet industry and signs of teacher domination—desks in rows and blackboard prominent; the other by rich but random materials, much talking, grouped

desks, movement, varying activity and a teacher largely sub-
merged in this activity. The justification question is complex.
For our purposes the important point is that there is not a
single level of justification. It is by now, I trust, clear that in
my view it is not for the philosopher himself ultimately to
justify but to indicate the areas in which justificatory arguments apply and to analyse their nature. Fundamentally each
teacher might argue that the atmosphere is justified because it
succeeds in promoting the educational ends—the learning—
aimed at. Then three questions should be asked:

1. Is the end justified? (either intrinsically or as a means
   to a further end).
2. Does the means in fact promote it? (empirical and instrumental).
3. What other results follow and what justification is there
   for these?

The first two questions would return us to now familiar
ground. The third is rather different for there is a change of
stress. The point is that it may well be argued that the 'atmosphere' itself is conveying certain values and building certain
attitudes. Indeed this seems undeniable. One could scarcely
teach that tidiness mattered in an atmosphere of constant un-
tidiness. The classrooms in our example are indicative of different priorities in the views of the teachers involved. Doubtless in justifying these there will be revealed differences in
learning aims and in teaching intentions. But the atmosphere
should not perhaps be seen as incidental. Many would maintain that much learning is absorbed directly from this—'learning by example' is a platitudinous phrase but an ever-present
reality.

The first of our two teachers clearly has views about his
pupils' relationship with one another and his with them. He is
unlikely to regard silent working as simply the best way in

which to learn certain things that he wishes to be learned but as valuable, important and necessary in itself. He does not support tidiness as an aid to learning alone but as a virtue. The second teacher is likely to wish children to communicate with one another not just because he argues that they learn better in this way but because he values this communication as such. The richness of the environment also is of importance to him in itself. Tidiness is of much less importance than stimulus. His own involvement within the class is not only a means to an end but is indicative of a view of human relationships, of the nature of the adult vis-à-vis the child.

Unless this is recognized, judgment will be made on a faulty basis. Some teachers may seek to justify their classroom atmosphere with arguments concerning learning effectiveness alone. Others may deny any value presuppositions and speak as though the atmosphere is neutral, though scarcely regarding it as negative. What is crucial is the recognition that the atmosphere of a classroom or a school reflects scales of values and views of what is of importance in life.

The concept of discipline is a particularly interesting one in this respect. Some teachers pride themselves upon being 'good disciplinarians'. Etymologically the word is rooted in the idea of 'discipuli', pupils. But it is a fallacy to suppose that a word 'really' means what it originally meant. It means what people who use it intend it to mean. Nevertheless consideration of origin is of value, for we may ask whether 'discipline' is best regarded as an end in itself or as a means to the end of helping the learning of the *discipuli*. One might point out, for example, that to have good discipline in a classroom is to have control of the situation in such a way that one's teaching objectives are not being hindered by factors such as inattention and misbehaviour. This of course would be a stipulative definition. But it would throw stress on discipline as a means to an end. In such a case the discipline might or might not involve quietness, lack of movement, instant obedience. It would depend upon the task in hand. The proof of the discipline would be in the learning. For many, however, such a view would be inadequate. They would hold that certain disciplinary features are intrinsically important. Some might argue that a noisy classroom was undesirable whatever learning took place.

'The good disciplinarian' referred to earlier is likely to hold that discipline, in his sense, is intrinsically good. One may suggest that any good teacher is necessarily a good disciplinarian if discipline is interpreted as the establishment of conditions appropriate for the intended learning. But many such would not use the phrase of themselves, for 'discipline', for them, is part of the background rather than the foreground of their teaching. By contrast those who pride themselves on their 'discipline' are very conscious of this feature of their work, as are their pupils. Might a case be made for suggesting that the best discipline is always unobtrusive?

Consideration of discipline frequently leads to discussion of punishment. Whether or not a disciplined situation is sustained by punishment or threat of punishment is a factual matter. And as punishment is thought of as, at best, a regrettable necessity (could it be thought of otherwise?) it is frequently asserted that the discipline is better if maintained without such punishment or such threat. There are of course many factual questions about the effectiveness of punishment—or its ineffectiveness—but these are not here our concern. What should be noted are several conceptual and logical points.

First it should be noted that from the fact that a particular punishment is effective it does not necessarily follow that it is justified. This is for two reasons. One is that the punishment itself may be thought inherently wrong, even if it does 'work'; the other is that even if it works it may not be necessary to success—to put it very simply, something else might work as well or better.

Secondly it is important to note that punishment, in most contexts, is conceptually connected with the notion of an offence. Children are punished in schools because they have committed some offence—or at least are thought to have done so. There are possible objections to this view. One is that we sometimes speak of a child 'taking a lot of punishment', for example from a bully. This however seems to be a looser and different sense of the term. We should certainly wish to distinguish it from that punishment imposed by someone in authority—with the authority, that is, to declare the offence to be such and to impose the punishment. Another objection might be the simple but pertinent one that a class is often punished for the offence of a member of it who has not 'owned up'. Clearly then many are being punished for offences which they have not committed. It would seem that we have to allow this extension.

It is important however not to lose sight of the principle of punishment as offence-linked. Many are inclined to see this as an old-fashioned view; retribution, they argue, is a thing of the past, a relic of a harsher age. The purpose of punishment is now seen clearly as deterrence or, more positively, reform. This argument is, I suggest, based on a misunderstanding: the punishment may indeed aim to deter (both the offender from repetition and others from action) and to reform, but it can only be inflicted if an offence has been committed. To do otherwise would be regarded as unjust. One does not punish someone who has done nothing wrong in order to deter him from doing something which one has good reason to suppose he is about to do. And it is not merely that such an action would be thought unjust but also, I suggest, that it would not be called a punishment at all.

Sometimes it is suggested that for someone to be punished a rule must have been broken. This seems to me at best misleading, at worst just wrong. It is wrong in the sense that children frequently are punished, without having broken a rule, if ordinary parlance is taken note of. A child will distinguish between being punished for running in the corridor when there is a known school rule forbidding this and being punished for disobeying Mr. X. The latter is not for breaking a rule. One could make the move from 'wrong' to 'misleading' by saying that it *is* breaking a rule, the rule that one should obey those in authority. I call this misleading because it seems to me so different as a rule from one which permanently prohibits a particular action that it does not belong in the same category. This is arguable but I prefer to go along with the child's distinction!

It may well be argued that these points are of far too high a degree of generality to be of prime concern to the teacher in practice. Yet it is important to note these general features as a background to particular decisions. For one can ask whether the following, as examples, are justifiable in the light of them:

i. the example quoted already—punishing the whole class because an offender has failed to own up
ii. punishing a child by making him repeat work which has been poorly done
iii. the infliction of corporal punishment

Let us consider these further.

(i) Why might this be done? The teacher presumably feels that the offender should not 'get away with it'. Sometimes it may be supposed that others in the class know who the offender is, but because 'telling tales' is against their code, (why?), are not revealing the information; in this case it may be hoped either that the threat of punishment will elicit the information required or that the offender will himself be 'punished' further by others in the class for getting them into trouble when they have done nothing wrong. There are differences in these situations and different questions arise. For example, is it ethically justifiable to try to force a child to act against the children's own ethical system of 'not splitting on one another'? Is it justifiable to create a situation in which children are set against one another? Is a group in any way responsible for the actions of its members? If some groups are so to be held responsible are all groups in the same position? Does the age of the children make any difference? Again our procedure is to break down the blanket issue into sections. Most questions of this kind are many questions wrapped up as one. They cannot be answered satisfactorily until the elements are disentangled and distinguished. At this stage there may simply be differences of judgment which cannot be reconciled; but at least it is known what the disagreement is about.

(ii) In this case it may be disputed whether this should count as punishment. It has been argued that as no more is involved than insistence that a task legitimately set be properly completed punishment simply does not come into it. Yet this logical-conceptual point is unlikely to make much appeal to the child who has the work to do again. Who is the teacher— or who is the philosopher—to say that the child's comment that 'I have to do it again as a punishment for being careless' is a misuse of language? It may be worth considering in practice the possibility that the degree to which it is seen by the child as a punishment might be in inverse proportion to the degree to which the proper completion of work is normally insisted upon. In other words, if it is known that work considered unsatisfactory is always returned may it not be viewed as simply part of the basic situation, while if it is normally just marked down but accepted the occasions of its return might be regarded as examples of punishment. This, however, is speculative.

(iii) In this area one can but sketch out a few basic points. First some may consider corporal punishment to be inherently wrong. If this view is consistently held as a basic principle it cannot, I think, be gainsaid by any argument. One may point out the practical consequences of holding such a position but if all are accepted by its proponents then the issue lies at a level where no further argument can resolve it. Once however it is allowed that such punishment may on occasion be justifiable then one is in the difficult position of trying to balance 'a choice of evils', to measure the implications of the punishment against the alleged beneficial consequences. The great problem in this area is that there is no general agreement regarding the measures involved. Indeed how could there be? The pain (and indignity?) of the punishment cannot be directly compared with the benefits of, for example, deterrence, because they are different kinds of thing with no common unit of measurement. We tend to use mathematical terminology here but this should not blind us to its imprecision; we speak of keeping the punishment in proportion to the offence but there is no measure of proportion. We are also plagued by many uncertainties regarding the facts. A punishment might succeed in deterring the offender but only at the expense of a rebellious undercurrent of feeling, leading perhaps to a deterioration in work. Was it then 'worth it'? The decision can only be an immediate one in the particular case. Unsatisfactory though it may seem, no simple guiding principle can be enunciated. One could say that punishment should be in proportion to the offence but this is an empty principle; no-one is likely to deny it but there will be much disagreement as to what is in fact proportionate.

To turn to the general nature of punishment, one further logical point seems to me to be important. That is that the existence of rules and an authority structure logically implies the existence of the possibility of punishment. Many will find this view unpalatable but it seems to be logically inescapable. I do not regard it as a value judgment. It can be expressed in this way. Suppose that a headmaster were to say of his school that it ran without any punishment whatsoever. He could maintain that rules were reasonable, generally agreed and universally followed, that commands by those in authority were always reasonable and justifiable, seen and recognized to be such, and obeyed. Now idyllic though this may seem, and sceptical though we might be, this is a situation which is logically possible. Suppose however one were to ask him what would happen *if* a pupil did break a rule or disobey a reasonable command and his answer were 'nothing at all'. Then, I suggest, one could maintain that the 'rule' was not a rule nor the 'command' a command. They might be pleas, requests, expectations, hopes but not rules or commands. One may of course then ask whether any institution could be rule or command free. And here I would suggest that although this might be logically possible it is in fact never so. And I am not at all sure even about the logical possibility—the reader may like to consider whether a rule-free institution might not be a contradiction in terms.

To many perhaps the whole issue of discipline, punishment, rules and commands may seem an unfortunate or unnecessary intrusion in a book on educational thinking. Freedom, it may be alleged, is the crucial precondition of healthy educational practice. Such a view tends to go along with the child-centred views discussed earlier.

Freedom is a hurrah word. One's response to it is positive. We prefer to be free rather than to be tied, restricted, impeded.

But there are other words which may also contrast with free which are not such boo words, for example 'organized', 'controlled', 'ordered'. When I say that these have not such a pejorative tone I am making an empirical generalization which could be false. Certainly I would agree that there may be some individuals for whom this is not the case.

The concept of freedom has been a central one in much philosophical discussion and again, in an introductory volume such as this, one can but make a few basic points and indicate possible approaches. Essentially, I suggest, 'free' is a word indicating degree rather than an either/or term, frequently though it may appear otherwise. Freedom is not something which we have or do not have but of which we have degrees. And we cannot sensibly maintain that children should or should not have it but only discuss thoughtfully how much of it they should have. Even this is misleading however, for in saying that it is a term of degree, and by referring to the amount of it that they should have, I am suggesting that it is a single quality or dimension. It is preferable to ask what are appropriate degrees of particular freedoms, linguistically artificial though this may sound.

It is clear that our freedom is limited in the first instance by physical possibility. I am not free to jump over a ten foot wall though I am free to try. Some would not wish to describe this as a limitation on freedom but this is a point we can by-pass. Having done so we see quickly that freedom is a concept with heavy social implications. What would be involved if I argued that because freedom is a good thing I should have the maximum possible? The consequence would be that I was freed from all social obligation. But in granting the same rights to others—and if freedom is good in general I must grant it as a right to others as well as to myself—I free them from any social obligation to me. If I am free not to pay taxes others are free not to educate my children; if I am free not to go to my place of employment others are free not to pay me. In one sense of course I am free in many such ways. I can simply not go to my place of employment. But my employers are free to seek redress in terms of a contract which they would say was binding upon me and which I *freely* entered into. Social cohesion depends necessarily upon recognized and accepted limitations upon one's freedom.

How do such considerations affect the question of the freedom of children in a class or a school? Immediately one says 'in a class or a school' one can ask whether the child is free not to be in the class or the school. And in British society anyway the answer is normally that he is not—there are, of course, particular issues in terms of children above the compulsory school age. Now if we grant that it is appropriate to limit the freedoms of parents by insisting that they send their children to school and of children by insisting that they attend, it would seem paradoxical then to claim that they should be free to do as they wish once in school. For presumably, in insisting that they should be at school, society is intending that the school should fulfil certain functions in respect of them. And along with this goes the right to limit their freedom in order that the functions may be fulfilled. Arguing this brings us to a frequent source of confusion. My point is that teachers have the right to limit the freedom of children in certain ways in order that educational purposes may be fulfilled (and, of course, for other reasons, for example mutual physical safety). This is quite distinct from asserting that in order for these purposes to be fulfilled a massive limitation of freedom must occur. The first is a logical point, the second an empirical one. The degree of curtailment of freedom necessary in order that particular purposes may be achieved remains an open question and one upon which evidence may be sought.

The 'progressive' and 'enlightened' primary school teacher who claims that he or she is quite capable of achieving the standards of work and behaviour thought desirable while leaving the children free to work as they please, is in fact engaged in work for which a claim is being made in the second area. What is being claimed is that the appropriate results can be obtained with a high level of choice for the children. But it is illusory to suppose that there is any acceptance of a position in which freedom is not limited at all. John is not allowed to hit Mary in order to further an experimental desire to discover how easily her nose bleeds. The children are not allowed to play ball on the main road which passes the school. They are not permitted to spend their school lunch money on sweets. Nor may they use their freedom to remain at school indefinitely rather than to return home when school is over.

A claim for freedom in schools is normally a claim for greater freedom in some particular area. And if it seems that I have been harsh on the 'progressives' I must reiterate that my objections are more to the misleading way in which some of them at times appear to describe their aims, intentions and methods than to their actual activities. In practice I normally find myself on their side.

The paradox of freedom is that if it is increased for someone it is often decreased for someone else. If a child is free to stay after school to finish a task upon which he is keenly engaged then his mother is not free to arrange for him to be at the hairdresser's ten minutes after school ends. If the school hall is free for any class at any time then no one class can know that it will be free for them to use at a given time. If all children are free to use the wendy house then the wendy house is not free for appropriate use when they all descend upon it. To generalize, society and civilization presuppose limitations upon individual freedom. A frequently quoted and very clear example from outside education is that of road traffic; the freedom of any individual motorist to drive exactly as he pleases is limited in order to allow traffic to move as freely as possible.

There is then no essential conflict between discipline and freedom in general terms. Far from being contradictory they are in fact complementary. Discipline and order create the boundaries within which particular freedoms operate. And the real questions to ask are not sweeping ones about whether the children are or are not to be free but in which ways it is appropriate for particular children to be free to do which things at which times. To many this may seem simply an evasion of an answer. But too much has often been asked of the expert in education. Teachers and parents have to make numerous individual decisions in particular cases. Analysis of what is involved is crucial but no answers will be found automatically to complex questions.

The link between freedom and discipline is frequently made through use of the concept of authority. Just as freedom has a positive emotive force so authority is frequently now thought to have developed a negative force. But our analysis so far, general and basic though it has been, should be sufficient to show that authority is a necessary feature of a social situation. It need not involve some of the unpleasant associations of arrogant superiority and passive obedience which often surround it, but as a feature of the social system it is unavoidable. Authority involves the right of one person to limit the freedom of others or the recognition by the others of some reason justifying obedience. The authority may be based on traditional ties and loyalties with no legal backing; in this case no sanction would follow disobedience to the commands of authority but time-honoured customs are regarded as binding. Thus the village schoolmaster was frequently regarded as exercising authority over those who had long since passed the stage at which he had any legal authority over them.

It is generally held that the traditional authority of the teacher is on the decline but tradition is not the sole source of his authority; he has also the backing of the law. He has the right to give certain commands and to impose sanctions if these are not obeyed. The actual facts of his rights and their limitations vary of course from society to society and are exceedingly complex. The 'crisis of authority' which is alleged to exist in schools comes from the fact that there seems to be a considerable gap between a teacher's legal authority and the authority which he requires in order to fulfil the tasks which society expects of him. Most teachers, however, would not in any case wish their relationship with their pupils to be based solely on the sanctions of law.

There are two other major elements in the concept of authority which may be involved in the teacher's position. One is that much of his authority derives from his knowledge and expertise. This may be officially endorsed by professional and academic qualifications; he may have the status of a qualified member of the teaching profession or hold a university degree. These are taken as signs that he has authority to teach in terms of his knowledge of how to do the job itself (if so mundane a word as job is not thought to be pejorative!) and of content, of subject matter. In some degree he is *in* authority because he is *an* authority. It is interesting that the possession of authority through knowledge has for long been thought sufficient for a teacher though this is now changing in Britain. There is however a sharp distinction between the official embodiment of such authority in qualifications and the actual recognition of it as existing by colleagues, parents and the children themselves—I make no claim for this being other than the most obvious of points! There is empirical evidence that children claim to place high priority upon a teacher 'knowing his subject and knowing how to teach'. Confidence in the teacher is closely linked with a readiness to recognize his authority. And in a very real sense one can ask why any child should be expected to accept the authority of a teacher who does not know what he is talking about (quite literally) or cannot help the child to learn. There may be institutional security at stake but for the child—and indeed for society—such a teacher is not fulfilling his role. The most basic form of a teacher's authority, it could be argued, is in his knowledge and his expertise.

The teacher may have authority too in another and more subjective sense. He may have personal authority, an authority conveyed by manner. Sometimes this is spoken of in terms suggesting showmanship of some sort; it is almost equated with 'personality' in the show-biz sense of the term. But it may come in much subtler forms. There is no doubt that some individuals seem to exercise an immediate authority in this sense, though the investigation of why this is so is not of course a matter for the philosopher. What is philosophically important is to recognize that this single word authority covers such a wide range of different aspects of a teacher's role. Even within personal authority it is vital to distinguish the immediately authoritative personality from the authority based upon a deepening relationship over time, that which involves the fact that children have come to know that a teacher can be trusted and relied upon. The acceptance of authority is then based upon respect. Yet the word 'respect' too has a range of nuances. A master who says 'the boys respect me' may be doing no more than using the word as a synonym for 'fear', but it might be the case that their respect for another master was based upon recognition of his personal qualities and conviction regarding his knowledge and teaching ability. He is

I

respected, his authority is respected and he is accepted as an authority.

Analysis of this kind has involved once again looking at an ordinary and well-known word in a range of familiar uses. But the effect should be to make us question the increasingly pejorative associations of the word mentioned at the outset. If it is alleged that 'authority is outdated'—and I have heard just this claim made—then the retort is 'which form of authority?' And if it is then alleged, seriously, that all forms of authority are outdated, the onus is on the person making the allegation to indicate what is to be put in their place. From the analysis of the concept the move is made to the substance of the situation. But this can only be described in words. And these may well lead back to 'authority' again.

Suppose, for example, that it be argued that authority is unnecessary if relationships are all based upon love. Love involves a concern and a respect for the other. And this in turn involves the recognition that the interests of the other may demand that freedoms be limited and authority be recognized. The question is not 'whether authority' but whose authority and what type of authority.

The difficulty of placing the emotive force of the word 'authority' is in interesting contrast to the clarity of the differences of emotive content in the terms 'authoritative' and 'authoritarian'. The former has a ring of confidence (if that phrase is not now so debased as to be unusable!) and contrasts with terms such as 'uncertain', 'bogus', or 'uninformed'. The latter suggests a shift towards the concept of power. The authoritarian teacher flaunts his authority, demands instant obedience, glories in superiority, discourages critical thought, treats evaluative questions as closed, . . . the reader may extend the list. But the earlier discussion should have shown that the concept of authority need not be associated with authoritarianism.

A further terms which may help to elucidate discussion of the inter-relationship of discipline, freedom and authority is 'responsibility'. 'Responsible' would seem to be either emotionally neutral or positive. Certainly to call someone irresponsible is to criticize them adversely—being irresponsible about something is quite different from not being responsible for it. At the simplest level to say that someone is responsible for something is to say no more than that he did it; John was responsible for spilling the ink may simply mean that John spilt the ink. But it may mean more. It may mean that, with care, he could have avoided doing so; that he acted irresponsibly. Or he may have spilt it without being held responsible, for example if Jim jogged his arm.

When one speaks of a teacher's responsibility for the children in his class one is using an umbrella term for a complex set of particular responsibilities. He may be responsible for them but he is not, in other senses, responsible for all that they do. It is even more difficult to generalize validly in this area than in most. Suppose, for example, that a teacher explains an arithmetical process to a group in his class. It is within their powers of comprehension; he explains it clearly; he takes adequate steps to ensure that they understand. In subsequent work one child makes a careless mistake. Now it would be quite absurd to suggest that the teacher was responsible for the mistake. Yet if a child were to make a careless mistake in apparatus work in the gym, following equal care by the teacher, the latter might well be held legally responsible for what occurred. It will be found by consideration of a range of examples that there are many subtle variations in what may be meant by the use of the same structure: 'X is responsible for Y'.

There are some general points which must be made nevertheless. Perhaps most important is to indicate that there is a conceptual link between authority and responsibility. If you make someone responsible for something it is logically absurd not to grant him the authority to carry through the responsibility, and this in turn, as we have seen, has implications for freedom. If a teacher is responsible for the distribution of exercise books in a school it follows that he must have the authority to stop his colleagues from helping themselves to them indiscriminately. This, I repeat, is a logical point.

Because it is logically absurd both to hold someone responsible in a situation and to give them no authority to carry through that responsibility it does not follow that there are no situations where this happens. Indeed the reader may well think of one affecting him—at which point my analysis here may have more impact than any other so far in convincing him that the analysis of concepts has practical implications! I can cite a personal example: I have had responsibility for securing school practice facilities for many students but without authority to insist upon being granted these. In practice a willingness to co-operate overcomes the gap but the position is nevertheless a logical absurdity.

Returning to the context of the classroom itself, problems in this area are frequently, I suspect, a cause of professional frustration and it may well help if they can be articulated more clearly. For example many teachers who are certainly not avenging and punitive by nature find themselves calling for further disciplinary powers almost despite themselves. May this not be because of the gap between that for which they are responsible and the authority to carry through the responsibility. Headteachers, parents and others hold the teacher responsible for order in the classroom but he finds his authority (of which kind?) inadequate to fulfil the responsibility.

We speak of responsibility not only in particular contexts but also as a characteristic of certain human beings. From the fact that X fulfils his responsibilities well in a number of different contexts we move to a description of X as a responsible person. And we tend to say that teachers must be responsible people and, further, that they must teach their pupils to be responsible.

An interesting feature of this is whether it makes sense to try to teach children to be responsible without giving them anything to be responsible for or about. One of the great strengths of what are often loosely called 'progressive methods' is that they normally involve a very great increase in the range of responsibilities of children. In formal methods the teacher holds to himself responsibility for the control of material and method. The sole responsibility of the child is to act within the bounds laid down. At times he scarcely has to be *responsive*, let alone responsible. Certainly he is unlikely to have much responsibility for anyone's actions other than his own.

But with freer methods, children become responsible for selection, planning and carrying through of work, often from a wide range of choices and over a considerable period of time. And often they share responsibility with and take responsibility for others. In a vertically grouped infant class for example there will be many opportunities for acceptance of such responsibilities. Even in this context, it may be noted, responsibility involves authority and the limitation of freedom. Does it make sense to say that Jane is responsible for handing out materials to her group unless it is implied also that she has the authority to do so and that the freedom of others to grab for themselves is denied?

A wide range of meanings may be implied when it is asserted that teachers should be responsible people or that children should be taught to be responsible. Some people wish to make the notion of reponsibility hold all their own particular views on morality and social custom. Thus some teachers may describe a newcomer to the profession as irresponsible because he has long hair and wears purple shirts. This, I would assert, is *not* an abuse of language. The implication is that one of the things for which the teacher is responsible is to set a good example to his pupils and his having long hair and wearing purple shirts is thought to constitute setting a bad example. The problem lies at the level of value differences about social custom rather than about views or responsibility as such. I would not hold that such a teacher was behaving irresponsibily but this is not because I think teachers have no obligation to set a good example but because I do not think that such a teacher is setting a bad example. In any dispute about this I should try to press the distinction between questions of social custom and questions of morality, but there is no set of arguments I—or anyone else—could produce which would finally settle the issue. If someone just holds these customs to be distasteful even if not ethically wrong, he does so. I may think him stupid but he is not irrational. And he has every right to think me stupid.

The exact balance of discipline, control, freedom, authority and responsibility in a classroom is found to vary from situation to situation, not only in the actual facts but in the ideal state. For 'ideal' is itself more of a relative than an absolute term though not normally recognized as such. If someone describes what is going on in a particular classroom as 'ideal' my response would be to say 'ideal for what or for whom?' And the argument would continue! This is not just because of an inherent awkwardness in my make-up, though perhaps this may at times go with an interest in philosophy! It is because the 'proper' situation in a classroom is one which is relative to many different aims and intentions in a dynamic situation. 'Ideal' suggests passivity all too easily. The classroom should be a place of activity and change and in its working all the aspects which we have discussed have their own subtle inter-connections.

These concepts arise as fundamental components in discussions of the school as a whole as they do in discussions of the classroom. One can properly ask for example, what are the respective responsibilities of a headteacher and of his staff. This can be asked as a factual question regarding a particular school. Or, again factually, it can be asked more generally; for example one might seek to know how Britain and the United States differed in their practice over division of responsibility. But one can also ask what are the appropriate divisions of responsibility. Similarly, one can enquire about the degree of authority that headteachers have or ought to have over members of their staff, or heads of departments over the members of their department. Or one can ask how much freedom an individual class or subject teacher has or should have over what he teaches. And it can be seen easily, that these sets of questions are not distinct from one another, because they involve concepts which are inter-connected.

It should now be clear, also, that answering the questions takes us still further; educational questions just refuse to remain in neat little boxes. In order to decide what degrees of freedom are appropriate for individual teachers, for example, we are taken straight into the realm of questions regarding how far objective answers can be produced to the question 'what should be taught?' which we have already to some extent discussed. So let us in fact leave these questions to further individual thought and move to consideration of just the same concepts in a still wider setting.

12. EDUCATION AND SOCIETY

Freedom, Authority and Responsibility

It is necessary to widen the perspective, for the school is not an isolated institution but one which operates within a complex system of social forces and which interacts with other institutions. Let us consider some of these before going on to questions regarding freedom, authority and so on within them.

First the school as an institution and teachers as professional people are deeply involved in political pressures and with political institutions. In Britain the central government as such owns no schools but the majority of schools are owned by local government authorities and administered by these. Central government however exercises general control over the system through the Secretary of State for Education and Science, the civil servants at the Department of Education and Science and Her Majesty's Inspectors. Many features of the educational system owe their origin and continuance to Parliamentary legislation. A change of political party in central government may produce new statute law affecting education or shifts in central policy.

The school will also be affected by changes in local control through the vote of the electorate in local government elections. Nor, of course, are such changes necessarily consonant with the central ones. At one point, for example, schools in Inner London had to work within a framework laid down by a Labour Secretary of State and a Conservative-controlled Education Committee. Six months later the reverse situation applied.

Local authorities frequently have inspectors and advisers also, these being politically independent. Boards of governors and managers contain both political and non-political representation. Many variations of pattern occur in the case of those schools which are not wholly maintained by local authorities, particularly those where a religious denomination still has a strong say in their control. With the details of these differences we are not here concerned; it is sufficient for present purposes to remind oneself that they exist.

From the fact, however, that the policies of central and local government impinge upon the schools, it by no means follows that the school should in all respects be servants of these masters. There may be areas in which the headmaster and/or staff should be those who take the key decisions. And what decisions should be made by parents? How far should parents be free to choose the schools to which their children go? And what authority have teachers or headteachers to give instructions to parents? And what are the appropriate freedoms of parents in respect of their children vis-à-vis the state and local government?

Inevitably I have moved from the varying factors and pressure groups in the educational system to their relationships with one another and, in so doing, am speaking immediately of freedom and authority and considering the balance of responsibilities. If in the microcosm of the school it was hard to generalize, we may expect it to be more difficult still in the macrocosm of society as a whole. Yet again some broad points may be made which will help to construct a framework enabling particular judgments to be seen in a fair perspective.

Perhaps the first of these should be that the paradox of freedom, referred to in the previous chapter, operates still more powerfully in the wider society. Let us consider just one claim, frequently made, involving the concept of freedom, namely that parents should be free to choose the school which their children attend. At first glance this seems a most reasonable claim. Indeed it might be thought of almost as a basic right. But it poses severe problems.

Suppose, initially, that the claim were made that this freedom is a basic right. Sometimes 'basic rights' are referred to as though they were inherent in the very nature of the human being. But we have seen already, in a different context, something of the difficulty caused by the idea of something being right because it is natural. The idea of rights presupposes rather than predates the existence of a regulated society. With no such society people may have opportunities, they do not have rights. A right to choose a school would have to be complemented by an obligation upon someone else's behalf to accept the choice. And it is this point, obvious enough when stated, that is frequently overlooked in practice.

Suppose, simply, that in a particular town there were three primary schools of approximately equal size. The local authority made no zoning arrangement, that is they did not allocate places on a geographical basis, but stated that parents had a free choice as to which school their children attended. Clearly it is likely that such a policy simply could not be followed through, for the distribution of choices could not be expected to match the distribution of places. Thus, in the very nature of the situation, some parents will be disappointed. And the disappointment reveals that the right to express a choice of which account is taken is not to be identified with the right to have the choice implemented. It must be emphasized that no-one is being perverse in this situation. It is simply that the social situation cannot guarantee the reconciliation of conflicting demands. And the demands of parents are conflicting if, in total, they exceed the supply of places available. Someone has to give way, or to be made to do so.

Again, I am aware that this seems very obvious. But the very fact that it is so obvious paradoxically seems often to obscure it. Many people speak as though the failure of administrators to devise a scheme in which parental choice is fully protected is a sign simply of bureaucratic inefficiency rather than something which is inevitable.

Given that total freedom of parental choice, far from being a basic right, is in fact illusory, how are the conflicts to be reconciled? The normal process is for those in authority, be they the local politicians, schoolteachers or officials of the education committee, to seek for relevant grounds upon which to make selection. And the discussion of relevance or irrelevance of grounds for decision is an issue with which philosophers are greatly concerned.

Let us turn then, for a time, to this issue of relevant reasons for decisions where the pursuit of individual freedom causes a clash of interests. It is frequently suggested that justice demands that if there is to be discrimination between two parties then there should be relevant grounds upon which the discrimination is based. I shall return to this point in more detail in the next chapter but its basic force can be seen even from watching children's play. If there seem to be no relevant grounds for a decision, that decision is often made by drawing lots or by the toss of a coin, or some such device. This involves tacit recognition that as no reason can be advanced to help resolve the situation, chance had best decide. Adult sophistication follows the same line; test cricket matches may in fact be heavily swayed by the winning of the toss yet how else is it to be decided which team shall bat first?

We tend to recoil, however, from allowing major personal decisions to be thus decided. In the case of choice of school it would be a simple enough matter to decide in this way. The names of all children entered for the school in question could be put 'in the hat', metaphorically if not literally, and a draw made. Why is this not done? Partly it seems to be because the matter is so important. But partly it is because one feels that if we were to search carefully we could find proper grounds upon which to make a decision. What might such grounds be? In order to answer this question we shall have to go a good deal further into examination of the concepts of equality and justice and this I intend to do in the next chapter. For the moment I leave it. But it was introduced here, and developed to this point, in order to show that as freedom for all is freedom for none and as we would be unwilling to accept arbitrary dictation from those in authority—at least I take it that we would —some way has to be found of reconciling differences.

Consider a further example where the concepts we are discussing are seen to inter-act. The members of an immigrant group wish their children to wear particular clothing for school on religious grounds. A headteacher, supported by the local authority, opposes this on grounds of the unsuitability of the dress for some of the activities in which the children are engaged. In support of their position the parents may claim freedom to have their children dressed as they wish. They may claim that it is their responsibility to bring up their children in accordance with the customs of their faith. They may claim that this is a proper discipline for the children. They may claim that their children are under their authority.

From the other side it may be claimed that the freedom of parents in respect of their children's dress is not absolute. In return for educational facilities they must abide by the regulations of the institution within which these facilities are provided. The Headteacher may claim that he has authority over the children when they are in school, that they are his responsibility, that it is in the interests of the discipline of the school that they should be made to conform to the same standards as other children.

The point which has perforce to be recognized is that no one side has a monopoly of the claims based upon these concepts. That a decision has to be made is clear, but no expertise on education can say which it should be. It is a repeated message of this book that analysis of situations again and again leaves the decisions open, for they may involve fundamental differences of evaluation which cannot wholly be resolved by rationality. Rationality is crucial in deciding exactly what the dispute is about but it will by no means always wholly resolve it.

A further example on a rather different plane: suppose that central government and local government clash on an issue of secondary school re-organization. I shall discuss later a number of points regarding this issue but one can ask now which voice should prevail. It is a matter of political fact in Britain that, in one sense, the voice of central government *could* prevail for statute law would be binding. Local authorities have the powers that they have because they have been granted them from the centre. But which voice *ought* to prevail? What general considerations could decide this issue? One might say that the authority which was putting forward the better plan should have its way but the point, of course, is that each thinks its own plan to be the better. One could perhaps say that if the local community think their plan better for them then they should have the right to decide. But how local is local? Can all small communities decide for themselves? Are there not advantages from overall planning and co-ordination? Have not those whose employment makes them geographically mobile an interest in the establishment of some degree of uniformity of plans and provision?

Take a further issue where freedom seems of paramount importance, namely the 'right' of parents to opt out of the maintained system of education completely and to purchase education for their children at independent schools on the open market at the going price. (Remark, incidentally, on the possible emotive effect—either way—of my choice of the language of capitalist economics at this point.) 'They are *our* children', parents may argue, 'not the state's. What authority has the state to forbid our educating them in the way in which we choose?' The reply is normally expressed—and this is crucial—not in terms of this freedom in itself being a bad thing but in terms of it clashing with another principle, that of social equality. To this again we shall return, but we may note now that the argument for freedom in and by itself, is likely to achieve nothing, any more than does an isolated argument based upon discipline, authority or responsibility. I can well imagine that this now reads as a wholly unnecessary underlining of the obvious. If this is so then I trust that it will be equally clear on the next occasion when an actual argument is heard beginning in a way similar to one of the following: 'this is a free country so I have every right to . . .'; 'no-one is going to tell me what to do with my own children . . .'; 'on whose authority do they think that they are . . .'; 'I'm responsible for him and if I say . . .'

In order to see further what freedoms should be permitted to whom and why, where authority should lie in the system, who should be held responsible for what, we shall have to see the principles we have been discussing not only in relation to one another but in relation to equality and within the context of democracy.

13. EDUCATION AND SOCIETY

Equality and Democracy

Twice so far we have been driven into consideration of the concept of equality, first, by implication, in consideration of relevant grounds for discrimination and, second, as a principle, 'social equality', which may run counter to the claims of freedom. Before considering these actual educational issues further it will be helpful to consider 'equality' itself.

In one of its senses it would not seem to be such as to arouse any emotive force at all. It is a mathematical expression. We say that two plus two equals four or that the sum of the angles of a triangle equals one hundred and eighty degrees. There are philosophical issues regarding the exact status of these claims but broadly we can say that, given certain definitions, they express mathematical truths. If we say that two children were equal tenth in an examination we mean no more and no less than that they gained the same numerical mark and that nine children gained higher marks.

The problem with which we are now faced is that of discovering the relationship between this mathematical concept and other uses of the term. Let us take the blanket claim that 'all men are equal'. Clearly this could be broken down into an equation which runs 'one man equals the next man equals the next man equals the next man ...' If this is done then one wants to say 'in what respect do they equal one another?' To which the obvious answer is 'in respect of being one man'. The argument has taken us nowhere. The reason for this is that the speaker who makes the claim is not using the term in its mathematical sense. Clearly all men are not wholly identical. Nor, it would seem, are there many respects in which they are identical—not, that is, if the respects which we are considering are observable characteristics.

The claim that all men are equal is sometimes expressed in religious terms, that they are equal 'in the sight of God'. For such a statement to be true then clearly there would have to be a God and man would have in fact to be seen as equal in his eyes (this, of course, being a metaphorical expression). But we should still, however great our faith, have to understand what was meant by the phrase, for, in respect of observable characteristics, men are no more equal in the sight of a postulated God than in the sight of men.

To claim that all men are equal is to make a judgment of value. To say that they are equal in the sight of God is to put forward a possible authoritative support for this value. The alleged equality is some form of equality of worth. It should be noted that I say 'some form' for in certain ways it is as obvious that men are of differing worth as that they are of differing height. What is being alleged is that their common manhood carries with it a presupposition that they should be proffered equal treatment unless—and we return to this point —relevant grounds can be educed for treating them differently. What is being put forward is, in a sense, an axiom for any system of treatment for one's fellow human beings: 'two human beings should be treated in the same way unless there are relevant grounds for treating them differently'.

It is possible to argue that such a presupposition underlies all our actions in this area, tacitly at any rate. The racialist does not deny it, he merely sees race as a relevant ground for discrimination where others see it as irrelevant. Even the dictator who sought to put himself first every time in the queue for consideration might well claim that he accepted the principle; it was simply that his leadership was in every instance a relevant ground for discrimination in his own favour! The argument would thus move from consideration of 'equality' to consideration of relevance.

This sense of equality is closely connected with our notion of justice. Justice involves two aspects, that of retribution and that of distribution. The first is the normal legal sense—already discussed to some extent—in which it is held to be just that an offender should be punished but is also held that justice demands that the punishment is proportionate to the offence. We noted earlier that 'proportion' is difficult to establish as there is no common measure for offences and punishments. (Is a £10 fine more in proportion than a £20 fine to the offence of driving a car without an M.O.T. certificate?) Distributive justice on the other hand is concerned simply with what we would normally call 'fair shares'. It is interesting that our mythical figure of justice (retributive) holds balanced scales. We see retributive justice as lying in a balance between offence and punishment, and distributive justice as involving the giving of equal shares unless there are good grounds for departing from equality. The proviso is of great importance. Distributive justice must not be equated with the giving of *equal* shares. To give equal shares of food to a starving beggar and to a gentleman who had just dined at the Hilton would be manifestly unjust—or at least any argument to the contrary would be likely to be highly critical of the Hilton!

In making this point however we are not wholly losing sight of our view of equality. For we should be making unequal provision in order to reduce an existing inequality. It is the opposite situation to that of 'to him that hath shall be given'. We perceive inequality and judge that justice demands that moves be made to reduce that inequality by a reversed inequality.

135

K

It is here that the notion of 'social equality' comes in. One who believes in a high degree of emphasis upon this principle, an egalitarian, is concerned not with greater equality of provision but with what I shall call a greater degree of 'end-state equality'. His notion of justice involves the view that a society with a great variation between individuals in wealth or opportunity or social esteem is *ipso facto* an unjust society. This statement needs some qualification however, for in making it as baldly as this I am suppressing distinctions within egalitarianism.

For example, some might wish to argue that the crucial area is one of equal opportunity. End-state inequalities are acceptable, it may be argued, without affront to the principle of justice, if and only if people have had the opportunity to keep up with their fellows. If their slipping behind is their own fault then society is, by definition, not to blame. Behind this lies a complex series of questions regarding the degree to which people are responsible for their own actions—questions which, traditionally, have been of great concern to philosophers—but these, in an introductory volume, we have perforce to leave. We can assume that a man is basically responsible for his own actions and at the same time throw doubt on whether the notion of equal opportunity is as straightforward as it may at first appear.

So vital is this concept in educational discussion that we must give it some detailed consideration even at an introductory level. Consider the analogy of a race. Each of the runners is at the starting line which is, quite properly, at right angles to the track, the finishing tape being likewise at right angles. Thus each has the same distance to run. Each lane of the track is of the same width, is made of the same material and is in good condition. No track has any obstacles in the way. Each runner can hear the starter equally well. No runner has weights to carry. In one sense therefore each runner has equal opportunity, that is to say the external task and conditions show no variations. But in another sense there are not equal opportunities. Some runners have had excellent training facilities and coaching, others none at all. Their diet has varied. Further they are of varying physique. Do any or all of these constitute variations in opportunity?

It is not an infrequent sight in school races with very young children to see a teacher, anxious to be fair, 'handicapping' the children in all kinds of ways, making an allowance for the younger ones and the physically smaller ones and the little boy whose knee has been bandaged. The interesting question, sympathetic though we may be with her motives, is that of what, in the end, the race is about. One is tempted to suppose that if she has done her job really well all the children will arrive at the tape at the same time! Or perhaps there is meant to be a differential element in effort—the hope being that the child who tries hardest will win.

Let us transfer the discussion back to the wider educational issue. Suppose it is argued that each child in our society should be given equal educational opportunity. What, precisely, could actually be the suggestion here? Certainly it sounds attractive; it appeals to our sense of justice. Of course everyone should have an equal chance. But what does this involve? One could create, at various points, an equality similar to that of the race where each one is level at the line and so on. In the process of selection for secondary education by an 11 + examination such an equality was established. I shall refer to it as 'formal equality'. Each child had the same test papers, the same length of time to do them in, a sharp pencil, often even identical chairs and desks. Everything was contrived for equality. Yet clearly the formal equality was matched by an equally clear 'substantial inequality'. This corresponds to the differences in training facilities, coaching and diet for the athletes in a race. Some of the children had been encouraged in their work at home, had been provided with books in the home, had had excellent play facilities through which they had learned. The quality of their language would relate to the pattern of linguistic usage in the home. Teaching and school facilities equally would vary from child to child. In sum, what was being tested was not simply the differences between the children but between the unequal opportunities with which they had already been provided.

We tend, therefore, to feel that formal equality is not enough, that it is insufficient to provide the 'true' equality of opportunity required. At this stage in the argument however great care is required. It will be noticed that I have referred to 'true' equality of opportunity, putting inverted commas in deliberately. It is a frequently used oratorical device in educational discussion, as elsewhere, to demand 'true' or 'real' equality or justice or opportunity or freedom or whatever. The implication is that there are bogus goods on offer masquerading under the name of the genuine article. We have seen however that there is nothing bogus about formal equality. It is an important and justifiable principle, regularly acted upon, and one can ascertain whether or not it exists. (It is quite a relief to be able to make such a positive statement!) Once however one moves away from it in the search for 'true' equality of opportunity one becomes increasingly unclear as to what one is searching for. Is it a mirage?

Let us return to the analogy of running a race. It will be remembered that in order to produce equality of opportunity right through, one abandoned, in effect, the notion of a race at all. I allowed the possibility of effort perhaps counting but it could clearly be argued that even this was a variable not wholly under the control of the competitor; some may have been encouraged at home to try their best and others discouraged.

The fact of the matter is that when we seek to reduce substantial inequalities by giving greater provision to those who, in the course of events, have had less, our actions are always a matter of more or less rather than either/or. It is not whether or not we make up the deficiencies but how far we do so. This is made the more so by the likelihood that there are innate genetic differences anyway (to this question we shall return later). Returning yet again to the race analogy, it will be recalled that I distinguished between training facilities, coaching, diet and variations of physique. Some of the latter, of course, would be genetic.

What is quite absurd, I am suggesting, is to suppose that it is the task of education to make up for all deficiencies, both environmental and, as far as possible by compensatory provision, genetic, in order to obtain a blanket end-state equality. To do this would be to try to produce the race in which everyone won.

It may here be argued that I am being dangerously misled (or dangerously misleading?) by the race analogy. In a race each competitor is striving for the same thing. Not everyone, however, seeks or requires the same benefits from education. This, of course, is true and the race analogy, like all analogies, points out only certain similarities between situations and is not intended to obliterate differences. Nevertheless many educational situations have been regarded as unjust though they allowed for varying opportunities.

For example, in Britain the 1944 Education Act provided that there should be secondary education for all according to three criteria, age, ability and aptitude. Here, it was thought by many, was equality of opportunity. The child of high general ability or high specific aptitude would be permitted, indeed encouraged to develop his ability or aptitude through the educational system and to reach the goals appropriate for him. What more could be required than this? More has been required by many. The idea foundered for two main reasons. One was the decreasing confidence of psychologists in their ability to measure innate ability or innate aptitudes. If this could not be done then the measured ability or aptitude already reflected existing inequalities. The second reason was that many felt that society should try to compensate in areas where a child lacked ability or aptitude if these areas either were thought to be of great educational value or were of great interest to the child.

I suggest that the egalitarian is in fact concerned with a view that all men matter, that every individual is, in some sense, of equal account. Thus, quite rightly in my view, he is highly reluctant to see children having options closed to them early, being 'fobbed off' with the third-rate, or being dismissed as hopeless because of the effects upon them of experiences and deprivations over which they have had no control. But this admirable attitude leads too often, through casual thinking and careless phraseology, to suggestions which would lead to a refusal to allow human differentiation as desirable at all.

This view brings us to another aspect of justice which has, I think, been much neglected of late. We speak a great deal both of retributive and of distributive justice, and the conceptual connections, which I have stressed, between justice and equality lead us to suppose, wrongly, that justice is always concerned with reducing inequalities. Why do I say 'wrongly'? I referred earlier to the Biblical 'to him that hath shall be given', with the implication that this is a notion of injustice. In many contexts it is simply this. But not in all. Suppose that a child reveals a particular talent at an early age. Would it be just to that child to deny it the opportunity to develop the talent even though the very development of it increases the inequalitites between the child and his peers in this respect? Frequently we say that children should work in such a way as to do justice to their gifts and it would seem to be equally necessary for us to do justice to them also. Our notion here, interestingly, still makes some use of the notion of equality, for we are saying that there should be provision roughly, at any rate, equal to the demand made upon us by the developing ability.

Thus, once again, we have seen that an apparently simple notion, that of equality, proves to be complex when more closely examined. The demands of equality are not identical with those of justice, though they are closely related to them, nor are either of these demands a single set upon a single dimension. To act justly by one individual may work against justice between individuals; to distribute scarce resources equally may satisfy none and leave injustice.

Our starting point for the discussion of justice and equality arose from considerations of freedom. It should now be clear that different principles which, taken in isolation, seem to be ones which we should wish to foster, clash with one another. The advocate of freedom can argue passionately in defence of fee-paying schools through appeal to the right of the individual to do as he wishes with his own money and for his own children. His opponent can reply, with equal passion, not through an attack upon freedom, but through appeal to what he may regard as the greater good—the equalization of opportunity. The philosopher cannot referee, but he can analyse the nature of the contest as I have to some extent, attempted to do.

In this instance there are further particular points which may be made. For example one could not envisage legislation which ruled out all inequality of provision for children. If two boys are studying Classics in a comprehensive school sixth-form in an all-maintained system the father of the one, who might otherwise have paid fees for his son, can hardly be prevented from arranging a long summer holiday in Greece, despite the fact that the other's father could not afford this. Nor can the 'learning benefit' of this be prevented, even if anyone were to think that it should be. On the other hand the principle of freedom need not necessarily be thought of as absolute. A government may certainly, if it wishes, enforce attendance at maintained schools or at schools 'licensed' in some way and argue the case in terms of the general good. After all, appeals to the general good are used as valid grounds for limitation of freedom in all societies. As pointed out earlier the very existence of governments is based upon the need to limit freedoms for wider benefits.

One may well ask whether any of the disputes which so bedevil education and educational politics could be resolved through the notion of democracy. Although, obviously the democratic basis of society may be questioned, is being questioned, and is only one of the possible forms of political organization, nevertheless it is broadly accepted by very many people and much argument presupposes the existence of a democratic structure. Can one deduce from the fact that such a structure exists that therefore certain values should predominate and thus, in turn, particular policies be followed?

It can reasonably be argued, in my view, that equality is the basic notion behind democracy. The slogan 'one man—one vote' epitomizes this. Democratic structures presume that all should have a say in those matters which affect all. Democracy further, I suggest, embodies the notion of a distinction between the expert's view on matters of fact and the right of all to judge on matters of value—a distinction to which frequent reference has been made throughout this book. Thus though many experts—demographers, economists, statisticians, military strategists, sociologists, town-planners, public health officials, etc. etc.—may advise government, the population as a whole ultimately choose policies; they evaluate the expertise without themselves being expert.

This is not a book on political theory but two caveats should perhaps be entered here. One is that I accept that there are massive difficulties in the working out of democratic principles in actual systems; the second that the word 'democracy', as all other such terms, has a wide range of possible definitions. Nevertheless, there would be a wide degree of agreement that the notion of equality is basic to it and that a democracy seeks to foster other values among which freedom is, perhaps, paramount.

Can, then, our view of democracy help us to reconcile the clashes of principles? Can democracy itself act as a sort of super-principle? My view is that it cannot. It could be argued that I have myself admitted that equality is given priority over freedom within the notion of democracy. Democracy both presupposes equality and, as a system of government, necessarily limits freedom. But it does not follow from this that when the principles again clash within the system equality must always prevail. Returning to the example of fee-paying schools it can be argued that they are out of place in a democracy only if the support of formal equality, pre-supposed by democracy, is extended into an attack on substantive inequalities—to assume that this is necessary, I have already argued, is to confuse two notions. We have here, I think, a straight clash of principles which rationality can help to clarify but cannot ultimately resolve.

From another aspect, however, the matter does not have to be left so much in the air, for though democracy cannot act as a super-principle it can give guidance on who is entitled to make decisions between conflicting principles. Care is needed here. To speak of a principle giving guidance is only a figure of speech. What I am asserting is that, given that the democratic basis of society is granted—and only on this presumption—it may be inferred that certain decisions rightly belong to certain groups in society.

At root, I would argue, the areas in which the principles of freedom and equality clash are areas in which democratic principles entail that the resolution of the clash should be through the ballot box. I suggested this in another context earlier. Frequently this is opposed as 'dragging education into politics'. The emotive force of this should be noted clearly. 'Education' it is implied, is good; 'politics' is being used with pejorative implications; 'dragging' implies the use of force, in this case to move something to a place where it does not belong. But if fundamental educational issues are crucial to society as a whole—and how can they be thought to be otherwise?—then it is central to democracy that decisions regarding them be made by society as a whole. And this entails political procedures.

It should not be inferred from this that the 'right' decision will emerge. The whole point is that frequently no one decision can be shown, indubitably, to be right. Nor, may we suppose, is the majority necessarily 'right', by whatever standards the rightness is judged. Yet any other way of reaching crucial decisions involves some form of action by authority. Of course the electorate may choose to delegate powers to authorities. But this is quite different in form from the exercise of power by any authority constituted outside democratic procedures. And arguments analogous to those used in discussing curriculum can be educed to show that teachers have no particular right to pronounce on the rightness or wrongness of the existence of independent schools.

A failure to resolve all value questions finally by rational argument seems to some to be a catastrophe. There is, however, no need for such a conclusion to lead to pessimism of any kind. Differences of opinion on these matters may lead to conflict but they may also co-exist peacefully and inter-act fruitfully. Consensus is often regarded as desirable. And we may agree that consensus on what is at issue is desirable in order that purposeful dialogue may ensue. But consensus on all issues might well lead to an impoverished society. Indeed if rationality could solve all problems the sole task for man would be to obey its dictates. I tend to rate choice, in many contexts, above consensus. But in saying this perhaps I am also re-establishing freedom vis-à-vis equality. How far is this so?—I leave the question as a rhetorical one.

If my analysis of democratic values has been anywhere near on the right lines—and I must stress again that it is my intention that the reader should be thinking critically about my arguments rather than merely accepting them—what implications are there for education itself? If certain features are crucial to education in a democracy how does one educate for democracy? I have argued repeatedly that it is not basically the professional task of the philosopher to pronounce on values but are there no values which the philosopher can underline?

There are, I believe, certain positive features which he may emphasize. The first is that the whole philosophical enterprise presupposes a readiness to accept the force of rational arguments to the limits to which they will go. If I am asked why this should be, I cannot answer, for, as indicated earlier, the question 'why?', in this type of context, presupposes rationality.

Secondly a recognition that 'rationality is not enough' should, I suggest, generate tolerance. It does not entail it. I might go so far with rationality and then rely on dogmatism.

Yet prudential, even if not ethical grounds, would suggest that this is unwise, for dogmatism can but clash with dogmatism and there are thus good reasons for being 'reasonable'—in the popular sense of the word. Certainly, to be personal for a moment, philosophical thinking has made me intolerant of intolerance but tolerant of many views which previously I might rather summarily have dismissed. Tolerance however should be confused neither with flabbiness nor with indifference. One may be personally convinced and passionately concerned yet still tolerant. And one should not confuse certitude—a state of mind, with certainty—a feature of propositions. There may be many things about which one *feels* certain but the truth of which one cannot prove. And, for me, one of these is that I should respect other people's feelings of certitude yet attack any attempt by them dogmatically to impose these upon others.

A democratic society therefore would do well to embody both rationality and tolerance in its schools; it would do well to encourage its future citizens to respect evidence and to question criteria, to listen to the expert but to watch that he does not blind them with his expertise and rob them of their rights of judgment.

14. FURTHER ISSUES

The discussion of issues in this book has ranged widely from the nature of the child to the structure of society. Throughout we have been concerned with clarifying the concepts which form the basis of educational discussion in order to help answer questions of justification of educational practice. I propose now to consider a few specific questions which have not hitherto loomed large in the discussion, though they may have been touched upon. In so doing there will be repetition of ways of thought already developed, for it is in the nature of philosophical thinking that structures of argument of very similar kinds may be developed within different contexts and content.

1. *The nature of intelligence*

It may, despite earlier discussions, seem slightly surprising that this topic is chosen. Prima facie it might seem that this is a subject for the psychologist rather than the philosopher. Philosophy however, in a sense, gave birth to psychology and has remained close to it in many respects. The crucial distinction between the two lies in the philosopher's concern with reasons, with justifications, and the psychologist's with causes, with explanations. But the philosopher is interested in concepts and the concepts which the psychologist uses are of no less interest to him than those of, for example, the politician.

So what may the philosopher say of intelligence? He may well note first that it is an abstract noun. Hardly a shattering observation. But an important one. Clearly it is linked with an equivalent adjective and adverb, 'intelligent' and 'intelligently'. Grammatically, 'intelligence' is something which a person possesses, to some degree, 'intelligent' is something which he is, to some degree, and 'intelligently' is a way in which he behaves, on some occasions. The adjectival use may also apply to a particular occasion for we may say 'that was an intelligent thing to do'. The move to the abstract noun suggests that a person does intelligent things, behaves intelligently, because of some *thing*, intelligence, which he possesses —or, perhaps, more or less of which he possesses. And this has led to attempts to measure how much of this thing he possesses. Philosophers, however, have become very cautious over our tendency to 'thingify'. They may point out, for example, that if we relate all remembering to the possession of some thing called a memory, we may be obscuring crucial distinctions. May not some people remember certain types of things well, e.g. visual images, and others different things, e.g. philosophical arguments. To speak of how good a memory a person has seems to be to obscure important distinctions.

So, perhaps, with intelligence. Do not people behave intelligently on some occasions and unintelligently on others, intelligently over certain kinds of matters and unintelligently over others? What justification could there be for lumping all occasions and all types of behaviour together as functions of one common intelligence? A psychologist may reply that, though no perfect correlation exists, nevertheless a tendency to behave intelligently on one occasion is likely to reflect general tendencies of this kind and that intelligent reaction to certain situations correlates with the likelihood of similar reaction to others. He may add that many situations have common features in any case and, further, that when a person who normally behaves intelligently on occasion fails to do so, the reason may lie not in some shortcoming in his mental capacity to respond intelligently but in the fact that emotional factors outweighed this. We do not, for example, necessarily hold it against a person's *intelligence* if he panics in a situation of extreme danger.

The philosopher can accept all this but still enter the caveat that recognition of these factors should lead to some caution regarding too blanket a use of the term. Frequently, however, the assertion has been made that the degree of a person's intelligence can be accurately measured and, moreover, that it can be shown to be an innate factor (though I hasten to add that the latter view, at any rate, is hardly current orthodoxy among psychologists). Let us take these points one at a time.

The psychologist is himself, qua psychologist, interested in technical problems of measurement. But the philosopher is interested in what it is to measure intelligence in any sense at all. What is being measured? Presumably it is a tendency to behave in certain ways in certain situations, or a capacity to do so. But this capacity cannot directly be observed. It can only be measured through measurement of behaviour, through measuring how intelligently people behave in particular situations. And when this is done there may always be features of the particular situation which distort the general pattern. The psychologist tends to regard this as a technical problem; it is to be overcome by repeated testing with different material and on different occasions in order to iron out the effects of the particularities. And, quite rightly, he can say that it is the correlation between these performances that gives rise to the supposition of a measurable capacity upon which they are all drawing.

The philosopher must still emphasize, however, that there are crucial distinctions between measuring intelligence and, for example, measuring height. Height is a single dimension and clearly measurable. Consider the statement 'this boy is really tall for his age but was not showing his height on this occasion'. Clearly this is nonsense. But it is not nonsense to say 'this boy is really intelligent for his age but was not showing his intelligence on this occasion'. In any test performance we can say that the result is itself an indication of achievement. If a pupil consistently scores above average then, barring the possibility of an extraordinary sequence of lucky guesses, clearly he has shown his capacity through his performance. Can we, however, infer absence of capacity from failure in performance? May it not be that latent capacity is present but that it has not yet been developed. This would seem, except in cases of brain damage or something of this kind, to be always a possibility. If a car passes me at 80 m.p.h. then it can go at 80 m.p.h.; if one passes me at 30 m.p.h. this does not mean that it cannot go at 80 m.p.h.

A measure of intelligence is thus a measure of performance from which a capacity is being inferred. How far could we then proceed to the argument that the capacity which is being measured is an innate capacity? A great deal of confusion has surrounded this notion, partly because of a tendency to assume that one can answer questions as worded without first questioning the question. For example, people sometimes simply ask the question 'is intelligence innate?'. Such a question suggests that there is a thing called intelligence which is wholly unambiguous and about which one can enquire 'is it innate?'. An odd point arises here however, for it may not be a factual question at all. Suppose that I were to define intelligence as 'innate general capacity'. Then no question arises. Intelligence is an innate factor because I have defined it as such.

Now obvious though this is—so obvious that it seems unnecessary almost to make the point—in it lies the source of much confusion, for many have defined it in this way and then proceeded to make various statements about intelligence which have gradually moved away from the stipulative definition with which they began. There is nothing wrong with this definition as such except, quite simply, that it is a stipulative and technical one. It is by no means necessarily what people mean when they normally use the term. The difficulty is seen particularly when it is enquired whether intelligence tests measure intelligence in the sense of innate general ability. The fascinating aspect of this is that in pursuing it we encounter two other topics which have been of much concern to us, yet which seem very different, namely equality of opportunity and the relationship between teaching and learning.

We must note first that many people have had strong reasons for wanting to believe that innate general ability could be measured. These arise from the notion of equality of opportunity. I implied, when discussing this earlier, that it would be an easier concept to handle if we could measure the abilities of those to whom we were giving opportunities. In Britain the 1944 Education Act sought to give equal opportunity to those of equal ability or aptitude. But it was required that the ability to be measured would be innate, for otherwise it would reflect existing differences of opportunity and thus the principle of justice would not fully be upheld. (It may even be thought that the concept of ability—unlike that of achievement—has that of 'innateness' already built in. This idea is supported by the fact that we normally speak of discovering ability as if it is just 'there'.)

The relationship between learning and teaching comes into the picture from the fact that it was thought by many that if you tested a child on material which he had not been taught then you would successfully measure ability which was innate. But this is not so. A child may learn from his environment without necessarily being taught. In fact any reaction to his environment at all, including the behaviour in intelligence tests, must necessarily reflect learning as well as innate ability. Of course the effects of learning will be greater in some areas than others but they cannot be eliminated.

Hereditary factors always inter-act with environmental ones. To some extent it may be possible to make some experimental estimates of proportionate degrees of hereditary and environmental influences—the problems here are technical and statistical (and they are highly complex)—but the philosopher can point out that to ask *of an individual* 'how much of his intelligence is due to his heredity and how much to his environment?' is like asking of a tulip 'how much of its development is due to what was in the bulb and how much to the soil, moisture, air and sunlight?'. The answer is that without both hereditary and environmental factors there would be no tulip. And in one sense intelligence is both one hundred per cent innate—there is nothing but the innate to develop—and one hundred per cent environmental—without an appropriate environment nothing develops.

One should note here too a fundamental ambiguity in the concept of environment which is often a source of confusion and which is very often wholly overlooked. Very frequently, as used by sociologists for example, it means the broad social context in which a person lives. For example people refer to a working-class environment. In this sense children within the same family clearly live in the same environment. But when it is 'paired' with heredity the intention is that the two terms are exclusive and exhaustive. That is, everything that affects a person's behaviour is either an inherited or an environmental factor and there is no overlap between them. Now, in this sense, a boy of ten and a girl of nine (to be specific) in one family would *not* have the same environment for the boy would have a younger sister in his environment and the girl an older brother in hers. And this is a significant difference! If all differences which are held not to be hereditary are thought of as environmental then no two people have the same environment. And it is environment in this sense, I suggest, which is at issue when intelligence is under discussion.

Thus, whenever the word 'intelligence' is encountered one must look most carefully at the context to see what it means. It has no *one* meaning, independent of use.

2. *How far can streaming be justified?*

In considering this question I am limiting myself again to constructing a framework of what is involved in answering it. I am not concerned with questions of the validity of statistics, with technical questions of measurement.

'Streaming' (or 'tracking' as it is called in the United States) is a device for grouping children into classes or groups for teaching purposes on the basis of their ability. Immediately one says this one recognizes that points from the previous discussion are relevant here also—but I will not repeat them. In order to pursue the question of whether it is a justifiable practice one can bring straight into play the intrinsic/instrumental distinction. This should now be familiar. Doing this alone is sufficient to show that disputants over streaming may simply be failing to connect. For some argue that it is wrong in itself and others try to dissuade them from their view by pointing to some alleged good effect. Clearly, however, this cannot work, for if the practice really is judged to be inherently wrong, no reference to good results will convince. By this I mean that the alleged good result can be accepted as in fact good by the other disputant without his abandoning his

L*

opposition to streaming. He may simply regard streaming as unethical in the light of our inability to measure innate ability.

Mostly however the arguments regarding it are instrumental ones. They are disputes regarding either the results to which it leads or the relative importance of differing results. I must distinguish clearly between these two aspects. A dispute regarding the results to which it leads is a dispute over the facts, over the evidence. And it is to be resolved by further evidence. A dispute in the second category is evaluative and may by no means be resolved by more knowledge of the facts.

Let us consider the factual dispute first. It could well be thought, from what has been argued hitherto, that philosophy has nothing to say about this. Evidence is not the philosopher's business. But there is one major point which should, I think, be raised. Procedurally, when one wishes to study the effects of any one factor, one seeks to hold other factors constant so that the differences concerned are solely the result of variations in the crucial area. For example if one wishes to discover the effect upon the growth of a particular plant of the presence or absence of a certain constituent from the soil, one sets up an experimental situation in which other factors are held constant. So, it might be thought, if one wishes to see the effects of streaming one simply sets up two situations, endeavouring to make them alike in all respects except that in the first case the pupils are streamed and in the second case they are not. The situation is by no means as simple as this however.

Let us return to the case of the plant. And let us suppose that the presence of the constituent in question is accompanied by better growth (whatever the agreed criteria for 'better' here may be). It does not follow from this that the results will always be better when this constituent is present but only (given that the experiment was repeated a number of times with the same result) that its presence is advantageous *in the conditions applying.* In some other set of conditions the addition of this constituent might have no effect at all or even be positively harmful. Thus a very wide range of experiments would have to be carried through before it could possibly be said that the constituent in question was always advantageous.

This, I suggest, is even more strongly the case with the testing of a variable such as streaming in education. Let us consider one other feature as an example. It may well be that an experimental situation in which certain types of teaching method are in use would show that streaming was advantageous (by the criteria agreed upon—we shall return to this) whereas if other methods were in use streaming would be shown to be disadvantageous by precisely the same set of criteria. Yet so often it is assumed that a question such as 'what are the results of streaming?' has a simple answer.

In order to test, in any given situation, the effect of streaming, it *is* necessary to isolate streaming/non-streaming as the single variable. Unfortunately however, one cannot proceed to argue that if the results with streaming are worse (again on agreed criteria) then non-streaming is desirable or vice versa. It may be the case that another factor in the situation is working directly against the success of streaming or against the success of non-streaming.

To be specific, it would seem reasonable to think it likely that the success or otherwise of streaming will vary with the teaching methods adopted. It would seem likely that the less class-based teaching there is, the greater is the likelihood of non-streaming succeeding, for clearly class-teaching would seem to be less appropriate the less homogeneous is the class. This hypothesis of course may be empirically tested, but for my present purposes it is sufficient to show that isolating the variable is inadequate as a test.

One may also note at this point that there may be different

results when testing *un*streaming from when testing *non*-streaming. In other words change itself is a variable. To show that B is superior to A is not, in itself, to show that movement from A to B will produce immediate good results; the change itself has to be taken into account.

These points, it will be remembered, are all concerned with endeavouring to show what are the results of changing a particular variable. But even if these problems are satisfactorily overcome it does not follow that agreement will be reached. For we have to return to consideration of the possibility of differing evaluation of the results. Throughout the foregoing discussion, I have been forced to assume that there are agreed criteria by which the results may be judged. But this is a false assumption.

Let us suppose that a particular experiment in unstreaming produced the following broad results (I emphasize that my argument here is wholly hypothetical; I am not for one moment speaking of any actual experimental results):

> the children appeared to be more outgoing and sociable; there was a general improvement in the level of spoken language, particularly among the less able; motivation to work was markedly improved among the less able but there was some decline in motivation among a few of the most able; attainment in 'basic skills' was little affected except for a marked falling off in arithmetical achievement among the more able.

Now *if* these were the results (and again I emphasize that the example is wholly my invention) there could be no automatic decision on whether or not to unstream. The evidence would simply be evidence; it would not generate a conclusion. Some might think the gains to be in important areas and the losses in unimportant ones and would thus cite the evidence as supporting the case for unstreaming. But the reverse argument would be equally logical. Each side could provide further arguments for its position, in terms perhaps of society's needs for people who communicate well orally or for the arithmetically able. But no argument will finally resolve the issue, for basic value differences may remain. This discussion may well serve as a general warning against all arguments which tell us that the facts demonstrate that undoubtedly some policy or other should be followed. Whenever we see or hear such an argument, we ought to search out the hidden value premises. It may be that we shall agree with these and, if satisfied with the technical status of the evidence, give our assent or support to the policies alleged to follow from it. But we should never do this without pulling out the value premises into the light of day.

Arguments about streaming are complex. They involve questions, for example, of how far individual injustices may be acceptable as a price for straightforward administration. And choices of this kind are unlikely to produce agreement. Some will take the view that no individual injustice is ever permissible if it can be righted. But they too should at least enquire at to the possible price of their view.

3. How should secondary education be organized?

The organization of secondary education has been one of the most controversial topics in educational discussion in England in recent years. We have already touched upon a number of points related to it in various contexts but it would seem to be worthwhile to draw these threads together and to consider other points which may be relevant to decision making in this area. Again, my concern is to explore the ground which has necessarily to be charted in order that the question may be answered and, yet again, it will be shown that no one answer can be demonstrated as right. The negative is well worth establishing for then discussion can appropriately continue with the recognition that differences of opinion are not necessarily the result of ignorance of the facts or of blind prejudice.

It is worth noting initially that giving a label to a school does not necessarily tell us much, if anything, about the nature of the institution. Thus 'modern' is a hurrah word, but 'secondary modern' did not thereby become a prestige term, for it was recognized that the 'modern' might have no force at all. To what, in any case, could it be intended to refer? Scarcely to the buildings in all cases. And methods are not made modern by labelling the school as modern. Nor can modern methods be necessarily equated with good methods. And, we might well ask, methods for achieving what?

A 'grammar' school at one time indicated something of its curriculum by the name. Clearly however this is now empty of content.

And what are we to make of the term 'comprehensive'? Clearly this too might be thought to have a positive emotive force; it suggests 'all-embracing' and can be contrasted with 'partial' and, perhaps, 'restrictive'. Yet what is 'comprehended' within it. The answer would seem to be 'the entire range of abilities'. But there are problems here. These are largely produced by the lack of social homogeneity of geographical areas. If the comprehensive school is to take in all the children of a particular area two points follow: firstly that the social composition of the school will reflect that of the area; second that the principle of freedom of choice will have been sacrificed (though it is of course true that, within economic limitations, people may freely choose where to live).

In this case the school will have within it the range of ability *within its area*, but this may well not reflect the general distribution of abilities in the country as a whole. The word 'comprehensive' may be applied to such a school but it may also be applied to schools where a mixture of parental choice and local administrative control (the latter phrase may be thought euphemistic) have produced a distribution of ability in each school within a wide area reflecting that of the area as a whole—each school, that is to say, being a rough cross-section of the area.

In actual fact the word 'comprehensive' may be applied to schools which conform to neither criterion, the area being 'creamed' of many able pupils into grammar and independent schools. One can infer very little indeed from the existence of a name.

Given this difficulty, however, what more may we say about the way in which the schooling should be organized? I would wish to repeat my earlier position that basic value differences must be resolved through political procedures in a democratic society, that the demand to keep politics out of education is a fundamentally misguided demand. If there is a clash between the principle of freedom and that of equality then it cannot be resolved by teachers or by educational researchers or by philosophers but only by the voters.

Nevertheless there is much that the educationist can say that is relevant to the decision. For example it is frequently maintained that comprehensive schools are preferable to a divided system on the grounds that they are likely to produce a less stratified adult society. For this argument to be an acceptable one in favour of comprehensive schools it is necessary (i) that one should want a less stratified society, there is nothing *illogical* in liking stratification though some think it unethical), and (ii) that there are reasonable grounds for holding that comprehensive schooling will in fact have this result. On the second point evidence may be sought, from the experience of other countries for example, or from research into the friendship patterns of pupils in comprehensive schools.

In general the argument is as complex as the range of criteria thought appropriate for judging educational success. In many ways the argument parallels that on streaming—divided schools can be thought of as super-streams—for there are the problems of seeing what in fact happens under various systems and problems of evaluating the results even if these are agreed. Variations in the system are likely to produce variations in academic standards (measured by . . .?), personal attitudes, pupil satisfaction, employer satisfaction, and . . . the reader may like to extend the list. And there are reasons for supposing that these variations in the results of differing systems will themselves vary further from pupil to pupil (or employer to employer or . . .?). Of course if it could be shown that any one system were uniformly superior for all individuals by all criteria then the issue would be settled. But this is a very tall order indeed.

It is my contention that differences of view on the organization of secondary education reflect, essentially, differences of view on what education as a whole is all about and these, in turn, reflect differences of view on what life as a whole is all about. Undoubtedly factual evidence may allay many fears and thus change opinions. If A's cherished criterion for judging educational success is satisfied for most pupils in grammar schools he may oppose comprehensivization. If shown that the same criterion is satisfied for even more children in a comprehensive system then he has no reason to maintain his opposition. But this hypothetical example assumes the existence of a clear criterion and of evidence which is valid. In fact we are a long way from firm evidence or agreed criteria and continued controversy must be expected.

4. *What is indoctrination?*

In discussing indoctrination, as in earlier issues, it is vital to stress the form of the argument used. One of the advantages of studying philosophy of education is that the skills developed are to some extent transferable. Methods which have been shown to be valuable in the analysis of one concept are likely to be proved fruitful when applied to other related concepts. And whereas the arrogance of thinking that one knows it all is the antithesis of the whole tone of this book, the confidence that one can make certain basic moves in structuring an argument is a confidence that it has sought to justify.

What, then, is indoctrination? What is X? 'Indoctrination' is a variable in a more generalized structure. And by now we should know that the dictionary is only of limited value and that there is not necessarily any one single right answer. Indoctrination means what people use it to mean and the emphasis of usage may shift. It cannot mean just anything. But there may be no exhaustive set of criteria for its proper use—for who is to judge what is proper?

Before seeking to answer 'what it is', within the bounds of freedom that the concept allows, it may be worth asking a linked question. Is it a bad thing? Or, expressed more precisely, does it follow that if something is correctly described as 'indoctrination' then it is to be regarded as undesirable? The odd aspect of this question is that it brings us straight back to one element in what the word means. For some people seem to use the word only for certain practices which they condemn. If they do this then the pejorative implication is actually part of the meaning of the word. This can be put in another way. For such a person the statement 'the process going on here is indoctrination but there is nothing wrong with it' would be a logical contradiction. It could not be true whatever was true of the process.

For others, however, it seems that 'indoctrination' is the name given to certain processes, the question of whether or not these are to be condemned remaining open. Thus, for such a person, to say that a process is indoctrinatory but acceptable may be rather surprising, but it is at least possible that, in certain circumstances, he would regard it as true.

What may be held to mark out the processes? Various suggestions have been put forward. Some wish to argue that indoctrination is essentially concerned with teaching as knowledge that which cannot be demonstrated to be true. For others this condition of 'controversiality' in the material is not necessarily to be regarded as part of the meaning of the term 'indoctrination'. For these, any person who seeks to implant any view in such a way that the learner never questions it is indoctrinating, regardless of the logical status of the view. Thus, for example, to ask whether one could indoctrinate a pupil with the view that Snowdon is the highest mountain in Wales seems only to be a question about the use of the word 'indoctrination'. Some would answer 'yes' and some 'no'; they use the word differently and neither I nor anyone else can referee. The vital point is simply to recognize that there is a difference between teaching truth without allowing questioning and teaching falsehood in the same way. And there is a distinction between teaching material the truth of which you can demonstrate and teaching, as if they were incontrovertible, views which you hold as a matter of faith or as a personal evaluation.

A further point arises with the question of whether or not

one can indoctrinate unintentionally. It seems clear that this is not actually a factual question but one of meaning, a semantic question. It is clear that, as a result of Mr. A's teaching, some children may come to believe in the truth of a view without questioning it, though Mr. A had no such intention. It is even possible that it is not even Mr. A's view! But it is disputable whether or not we wish to call this indoctrination.

It may well be thought—I do think this—that the issue of how we use the word is of importance solely because, unless we are clear, we may misunderstand what is at stake in a case where clearly there are vital points of substance. But we cannot solve the problem by legislating once-and-for-all, context-free criteria for 'indoctrination' but only by exploring patiently what is being alleged in detail when the word is used. And one may note that an appeal to etymology is not conclusive (this, too, is a point we have encountered before). From the fact that originally the word is connected with the passing on of doctrine it does not follow that it can now be correctly used only in this sense. And, even if it were to follow, the word 'doctrine' itself has no single, clear and unambiguous meaning.

Let us then move from the troubles that consideration of the word produces and ask the question of substance which, centrally, seems to lie behind it. Do we wish to condemn methods which, intentionally or unintentionally, transmit material in such a way that it is unquestioned. Some may then answer a blanket 'yes'. Others may say 'only if it is controversial material'. Yet others may say 'only if it is controversial material over which I hold a different view'! And to decide between these positions is likely to lead far beyond the narrower confines of educational institutions and into our total view of life. This is consonant with a general position adopted in this book, that educational questions, probed at depth, turn out to be fundamental questions about life and its purposes.

Personally, I have a deep-rooted and intense hatred (the word is chosen advisedly) of all attempts to implant religious or political views in such a way as to prohibit, if possible, or discourage the questioning of these. To act in this way I regard as anti-educative, unethical, and damaging of the fundamental 'personhood' of the pupil. This is a value judgment of mine. But I cannot persuade others to share it by arguing 'this is indoctrination', 'indoctrination is wrong', therefore 'this is wrong'. In other words a point of semantic usage, of the meaning of a word, cannot generate a value position. People simply have to decide whether or not they regard such a process as wrong. I cannot 'prove it wrong'. I do not know what it could mean to *prove* it wrong, passionately though I hold it to be wrong.

This does not mean that 'my view is as good as anyone else's'. I can argue for my view against someone else's by appealing to the intrinsic nature of the indoctrinatory process or by discussing the results of it.

For example, I may point out that if one person uses methods which by-pass or obliterate rationality in order to press his values on others then he must allow others with different views to do likewise. It may be objected that only 'the right views' or 'true values' should be passed on in this way, but one must then point out the lack of agreement on these. If it is still alleged that there is a right in one instance but not in the other then rationality is itself being outraged and no further rational move can be conclusive. If this happens then the issue may unfortunately be resolved by power rather than reason.

It is sometimes suggested that indoctrination is a necessary part of the education of young children. Granted that their powers of reason are undeveloped, the argument runs, they must be taught without reason fully being taken into account. Habits of behaviour must be instilled without these being able to be questioned. The point to notice here is that if such processes are necessary and if they are called indoctrination then indoctrination cannot be condemned as such; for what is the point of condemning action which is unavoidable? It would seem more sensible here to build in the intention criterion to our concept of indoctrination and to say that processes with young children are not indoctrinatory if the teacher is willing that, when reasoning powers have been developed, that which has been learned should be called into question. But in saying this I am stipulating a condition of usage (though not arbitrarily—I state my reason) which not all may wish to follow.

When a protagonist in an argument thunders forth 'this is not education, it is indoctrination', his choice of words proves nothing of itself. One has to ask first what features of the process in question are being described as indoctrinatory, why they are being so described, and whether and for what reasons one wishes to condemn them. Strong language is no substitute for clear thought.

15. CONCLUSION

In one important sense this book has no conclusions. It should end with a row of dots . . . . the argument continues. It has been concerned with ways of looking at educational issues. The assumption has been that the reader wishes to be helped to make informed judgments about these. 'Informed' involves knowledge of the facts. These must be ascertained elsewhere. This book has been concerned with the judgment. During the course of it I have made judgments myself. But these are all open to question. This is true not only of any tentative conclusions I have come to in particular arguments but of any presuppositions of my argument.

I have, for example, placed heavy stress on the meaning of a term being context-dependent. How far am I justified in this? Have I exaggerated perhaps? Further reading and thought may lead the reader to give further attention to this area.

I have placed heavy stress on the distinction between facts and values and on the relativity of value judgments. But the arguments I have used have involved a degree of simplification inevitable in an introductory volume. Certainly I have 'used' certain concepts implying positive evaluation. I have assumed for example that freedom and justice matter, though I have argued for the complexity of what they involve and the immense difficulty of resolving particular conflicts where fundamental principles appear to clash. And I have assumed the value of rationality.

If I am thought to be mistaken in any of my judgments I must stress yet again that I have argued throughout the book that rational argument is open. Counter arguments may be put to mine. But the very process of reading the book should have helped the formulation of such arguments.

Controversial points in my own argument can be enlarged upon by using against me the methods which I have used. If an author cites unreliable evidence the reader is powerless unless he checks elsewhere. But philosophical arguments may be countered within their own terms.

Certainly it is vital to recognize that in no discussion do I make any claim to have analysed any issue or the use of any concept exhaustively. The volume is, by its nature, no more than introductory. In each area discussed only selected points have been made and only certain usages examined. To repeat an earlier point, I have been concerned with a way in. Much more can pertinently be said in every area entered. There has been no attempt to construct detailed maps in any area. And I recognize that my selection of points is always open to argument.

No reader should rely too much on any one introductory volume. Further suggestions for reading are made in the brief bibliography which follows. But philosophizing is an activity which should not be generated by books on philosophy alone. The ways of thinking that have been the subject of this book are central to all educational judgment; they should help the reader in considering statements by politicians and self-appointed educational pundits, by speakers at Parent–Teacher meetings and by contributors to newspaper correspondence columns, in common-room conversations and in informal discussions. If the book makes a contribution to clearer thinking about education it will have fulfilled its purpose. For it is my conviction that greater clarity of thought can help sound judgment and, as a consequence, lead to more justifiable practice.

BIBLIOGRAPHY

An excellent introduction to the activity of philosophizing in general is:
Emmet, E. R. *Learning to Philosophize* (Penguin Books, 1968).

General introductions to Philosophy of Education include:
Gribble, J. *Introduction to Philosophy of Education* (Allyn and Bacon, 1969).
Langford, G. *Philosophy and Education: An Introduction* (Macmillan, 1968).
O'Connor, D. J. *An Introduction to the Philosophy of Education* (Routledge and Kegan Paul, 1967). (A seminal book with a strongly indentifiable view of Philosophy.)
Peters, R. S. and Hirst, P. H. *The Logic of Education* (Routledge and Kegan Paul, 1970). (A book of great importance, arguing for the nature of the educational process as closely related to the nature of knowledge.)
Soltis, J. F. *An Introduction to the Analysis of Educational Concepts* (Addison Wesley, 1968).

A number of points of great interest are lucidly discussed in
Peters, R. S. *Authority, Responsibility and Education* (Allen and Unwin, 1959).

More difficult but vitally important for understanding at depth is
Peters, R. S. *Ethics and Education* (Allen and Unwin, 1966).

168

Of wide interest is:

Dearden, R. F. *The Philosophy of Primary Education* (Routledge and Kegan Paul, 1968).

Close analysis of great importance is contained in:

Wilson, P. S. *Interest and Discipline in Education* (Routledge and Kegan Paul, 1971).

Interesting and important collections of papers are:

Archambault, R. D. (ed.) *Philosophical Analysis and Education* (Routledge and Kegan Paul, 1965).

Peters, R. S. (ed.) *The Concept of Education* (Routledge and Kegan Paul, 1967).

Hollins, T. H. B. (ed.) *Aims in Education: The Philosophic Approach* (Manchester U. P., 1964).

A more detailed bibliography will be found in *The Logic of Education* (see above).

For the fullest references see:

Powell, J. P. *Philosophy of Education: A select bibliography* (Manchester U. P., 1970).